Gregory W. Engle
Tibor P. Nagy

Managing Overseas Operations: Kiss Your Latte Goodbye

This book is typeset in Bookman Old Style. The paper
used in this book meets the specifications for 60# white
444ppi.

Cover design by Summer Sutton
Illustrations by Dusty Higgins

ISBN-10: 0983802467 (paperback)
ISBN-13: 978-0-9838024-6-4 (paperback)

Printed and Manufactured in the United States of America
First printing, 2012
Typeset in the U.S.A.

Published and distributed in North America by
Vargas Publishing
P.O. Box 6801
Lubbock, TX 79461
http://www.vargaspublishing.com

To Maureen, Jessica and Ryan, the best mobile support team an international manager could have.

To Stephen, Tisza, Peter – and most especially Jane – for not just enduring, but always thriving, even in the most difficult of circumstances.

Appointment Calendar

All-day event: *Consultations with Ambassadors Nagy and Engle*

About the Authors

Ambassador Gregory W. Engle (Ret)

Ambassador Engle is currently serving as Peace Corps Country Director in Ethiopia. Previously he was the U.S. Department of State's Diplomat-in-Residence at the Lyndon B. Johnson School of Public Affairs, The University of Texas at Austin. Subsequent to his retirement from the Foreign Service in 2008, he served as Senior Advisor for International Affairs at The University of Texas International Office, and thereafter as Associate Director of the University's Robert S. Strauss Center for International Security and Law.

A career diplomat and Foreign Service officer with extensive international management and policy experience, Ambassador Engle has a vast portfolio of distinguished service. While on a thirteen-month assignment as Management Counselor of the U.S. Embassy in Baghdad, Iraq, he managed a full range of administrative functions and oversaw the provision of $450 million of life support services for the United States' largest diplomatic mission. Before serving in Iraq, Ambassador Engle was the U.S. ambassador to the Togolese Republic, where he primarily focused on promoting representative government and greater respect for human rights.

Ambassador Engle joined the Foreign Service (U.S. Department of State) in 1981, following a tour as a Peace Corps

Volunteer in South Korea. He served in management positions in Pakistan, Germany, Washington, Ethiopia and Cyprus. He was the recipient of the State Department's prestigious Leamon R. Hunt Award for Administrative Excellence for his service in Ethiopia, in part for his role in the search and recovery mission that followed the plane crash that killed Texas Congressman Mickey Leland and 18 other Americans and Ethiopians. Following his assignment in Cyprus, Ambassador Engle served as Deputy Chief of Mission at the U.S. Embassy in Lilongwe, Malawi, from 1992 to 1995, during which that country made its transition from decades of one-man rule to a democratically elected government. From 1996 to 1999, he was U.S. Consul General in Johannesburg, South Africa.

Upon his return to Washington, Ambassador Engle served as Director of International Cooperative Administrative Support Services (ICASS) from 1999 to 2001, Special Coordinator for the African Crisis Response Initiative from 2001 to 2002, and Director of the Office of Regional and Security Affairs in the State Department's Bureau of African Affairs from 2002 to 2003.

Ambassador Tibor P. Nagy, Jr. (Ret.)

Ambassador Tibor P. Nagy, Jr. is currently serving as Vice Provost for International Affairs at Texas Tech University.

During the 2002 academic year he was the Department of State's "Diplomat in Residence" at the University of Oklahoma. Previously he was the U.S. ambassador to Ethiopia from 1999-2002, and ambassador to Guinea from 1996-99. Before that, he attended the Department of State's prestigious Senior Seminar. During this year, Ambassador Nagy lectured extensively at educational institutions and to civic groups around the U.S. about US foreign policy, Africa, diplomatic careers and Foreign Service life.

Ambassador Nagy joined the Foreign Service in 1978 as a management analyst in the Bureau of Personnel. His first overseas assignment was as General Services Officer in Lusaka, Zambia from 1979-81. After that, he was assigned to Victoria, Seychelles, for two years as Administrative Officer. He served as Systems Administrator for the African Bureau in Washington from 1983-84 and then returned overseas as Administrative

Officer in Addis Ababa, Ethiopia from 1984-86. For the next eight years, he was Deputy Chief of Mission at Lomé, Togo (1987-90); Yaounde, Cameroon (1990-93); and Lagos, Nigeria (1993-95).

Ambassador Nagy was born in Budapest, Hungary on April 29, 1949 and arrived in the United States as a political refugee in 1957. He received a B.A. from Texas Tech University in 1972 and an M.S.A. from George Washington University in 1978. He speaks Hungarian and French, and has received numerous awards, including the Department of State's "Superior Honor" award, five "Meritorious Honor" awards as well as being runner-up for the prestigious "Deputy Chief of Mission of the Year" award. He was also knighted by the President of Guinea.

Introduction

Perhaps you're sitting on a plane headed for your first management position overseas. Even more ideally, you're still at headquarters preparing for that assignment. Or you're assigned to headquarters and you are responsible for providing support to your organization's overseas operations. Maybe you're a student taking a course in international management or administration. Or perhaps you have already served in positions with management responsibilities overseas, and you're determined to figure out how your organization can better implement its programs and achieve its objectives.

Whatever the case may be, you've picked up this book because you want to learn more about managing an organization in a foreign environment. Is it really that different from managing an organization in the United States or the country from which you come? If so, what are the differences? What are the factors that determine the success or failure of someone managing an overseas operation? What skills and knowledge are essential to addressing these factors? How can you develop them? If you're going to head up the overseas operation or one of its program units, how much of this stuff do you really need to know? Aren't there others -- management officers, for instance -- you can rely upon to deal with such matters?

Managing Overseas Is Different

Managing an organization overseas *is* different. That is not to say that the management skills you've developed to direct operations in your own country will not apply in a foreign location. They should still serve you well. Understanding the fundamentals of leadership is vital to the success of a manager at home or abroad. Basic knowledge of strategic planning and implementation, financial operations, human resource management, inventory operations, procurement and contracting, logistics, information management and technology, and security operations is likewise important to those who bear responsibility for managing these functions overseas or in support of overseas operations.

The skills and knowledge you need to be an effective manager in your own country might account (unscientifically and hypothetically) for 80 percent of what you need to know to be an effective manager overseas, so obviously, you have to bring them with you. But the remaining 20 percent of what you need to know – that which is unique to managing overseas -- will be vital to your success. The authors have observed many cases in which individuals have failed in their overseas management assignments, often curtailing their overseas tour of duty at their own request or the organization's. Generally these people have had the requisite technical skills to perform the jobs to which the organization has assigned them, but they have lacked the unique knowledge, understanding and temperament required to be an effective manager overseas.

So what constitutes that critical 20 percent (or 15, 25, 30 percent)? At the most obvious level, it is the foreign culture and environment: The people in the country to which you have been assigned are not like you in many respects. They probably speak a different language or languages; they have a different concept of time, or perhaps *no* respect for time, from your perspective; they say "yes" when they mean "no." In the workplace, they don't expect their boss to solicit their opinions about how something should be done -- or maybe they expect their boss to consult with them in *every* case before taking action. The political system is different, perhaps corrupt and non-democratic. Likewise, the judicial system is not what you're accustomed to, and people seem to have very different attitudes about what constitutes a commitment or legal obligation in business transactions. If you report to your assignment uninformed about the culture of the country in which it is located, you're in big trouble.

But the differences go beyond culture. Some differences are purely practical and require practical responses. For heaven sakes, *these* people drive on the wrong side of the road! What does that mean about the types of vehicles your organization requires? What if your organization has rules that require its overseas operations to buy vehicles from the home country (as the U.S. Government required of its diplomatic posts until fairly recently)? Your country of assignment will use a different monetary unit or currency, and the rate of exchange between that currency and the currency your organization's headquarters uses for its financial operations will fluctuate. If the value of your organization's currency drops against that of the country of your assignment, you will lose buying power. How will you ensure that you have the funds you need to operate? And your office overseas will very likely have at least two types of employees: those who are from the country where the office is located and those who are not. Are they on the same pay and benefit plans? Very often they are not. If that is the case, are there tensions and jealousies between these groups of employees? Be prepared!

International Management is a Growth Industry

International management is a growth industry in all sectors: public, private and nonprofit. Globalization has definitely hit the labor market. There is a growing number of jobs overseas for those with an interest in international relations and national security, development work, human rights, journalism, international business, global climate and environmental issues, missionary work and a full range of other pursuits. In fact, the opportunity to serve overseas is not only growing, but in many fields people are obligated to take an international assignment as a condition of employment or career advancement. Very often, those who take positions overseas will work for organizations that are themselves foreign to the country to which the individual is assigned. These organizations need international managers for their expanding global operations.

And guess what? Global really means global. Long gone are the days when one could spend an international career moving among the capitals of Europe, the Far East or a few posh and exotic spots in Latin America. The rugged outposts of the world – the less developed countries and emerging markets in which 75 percent of the world's population lives -- are the new "lands of opportunity," and today's international manager has to be adept at navigating their unpredictable and sometimes treacherous waters.

The good news, if you relish a professional challenge, is that many of these tougher locations are among the most rewarding places to work. Scoring the important diplomatic success, landing the big contract, or bringing vital new services to the poor under very harsh conditions is a major achievement, and many international managers – some of them "crisis junkies" – are extremely motivated by such challenges. But even beyond the great satisfaction of achieving your organization's goals, the actions you take as a manager in such places will often have a more profound impact (positive, one hopes) on those who work for you and those your unit serves than would likely be the case in the more predictable and secure environment of a developed country. In a poor country, characterized by high unemployment and an unstable economy, the opportunities for training and advancement that you can offer your local employees on behalf of your organization will be hard for them to

4

find anywhere else, and your ability to help them develop their careers will be considerable. That is certainly something a good manager can value and take pride in, especially when you consider that the person you hire, develop and promote in a poor country is normally supporting not four or five other family members, but rather 15 or 20 in his or her extended family. We'll say more about the challenges and rewards of managing local employees in different countries later.

Managing Expectations

So how can this book help you be a more effective manager overseas? To answer this question, we need to be explicit about the book's scope and focus and certain biases the authors bring to the subject.

The focus of this book is *management* of an organization overseas. It will not address the goals or objectives of any particular type of organization. It is *not* about foreign policy, international business strategy, or the development objectives of international organizations and nongovernmental organizations (NGOs). It *is* about establishing and fostering sound internal management policies and practices and a strong administrative platform to better ensure that the organization, whatever its unique goals and objectives might be, achieves them.

Although many of the management principles and practices addressed in this book are equally applicable to both public and private sector organizations, the book's principal focus will be on the former. In this case, we use the term "public sector" broadly to include governmental, international and nongovernmental or nonprofit organizations. There are many books about "international management" on the market, and almost all of them concern international *business* management and strategy, with an emphasis on competing in the global marketplace. Public sector organizations, as we have broadly defined them, are not really in the business of competing with one another in the same sense that commercial firms do. Thus, while some of what has been written about international business management is relevant to those who manage public sector organizations in foreign locations, there is also much that is not.

5

What little literature there is about international *public sector* management tends to fall into two or three categories: It is often specific to one organization or family of organizations, such as the United Nations system; it is comparative rather than international, examining and contrasting different countries' government structures and administrative systems; or, especially where it is referred to as "international administration," it concerns external program implementation. This book is somewhat unique in its focus on the internal management and administrative functions that are applicable to the broad range of public sector organizations that have operations in countries beyond those in which their headquarters are located.

This is not a textbook. You will not find much in the way of theories, research or even sources cited on these pages. It is, first and foremost, a book *for* practitioners written *by* practitioners. The authors have more than 50 years of collective experience in managing international operations. Almost all of the information, insights and guidance we offer come directly from our own experience or the experiences of the many international managers we have interacted with over the course of our careers. We want to provide you, the current or future international manager, with some practical things to think about and some ways to think about them as you approach the challenge of managing an overseas operation. As the previous section intimated, you will also find a certain bias for addressing management challenges that one encounters in the out-of-the-way, often poor, unstable and unpredictable new frontier of the international manager: overseas operations in developing and emerging countries.

The book is for the management or executive officer of overseas operations, but it is also for any member of the expatriate staff (i.e., not of the host country) who bears responsibility for managing personnel and other resources or supervises people who do. In fact, overseas operations come in many sizes and shapes, and many of them do not have a management or executive officer. NGOs, even very large ones, often assign only one expatriate or international staff member to a country office. That person is responsible for implementing the NGO's programs, but is also going to spend a considerable portion of his or her time dealing with internal management and administrative matters. Many diplomatic missions will have a

6

management officer, but that doesn't absolve the ambassador of the responsibility to understand how the embassy operates, what is important to its local and expatriate staff, or whether or not the mission has received adequate funding and is getting the support it needs from headquarters. Heads of embassies and other types of overseas operations who lack a basic understanding of how the place operates are often not very effective in using the organization's resources to advance the policies or achieve the goals that they might understand very well.

Defining Some Terms

The practice of international management is perhaps less burdened with specialized terminology than many other fields. There is some, to be sure, and where we employ it, we generally do so in context. A few terms and concepts, however, warrant a definition or explanation at the outset.

International management: Managing an organization in a country other than the one in which the headquarters of the organization is located *or* managing an international or regional organization or a unit within it, wherever it is located. One could imagine many definitions of "international management," but we use this one to make the point that the *organization*, not simply those who manage it, is foreign to the country where it is operating. It is the "foreignness" of the organization that leads to many of the unique challenges of managing it.

International manager: An individual who manages an organization in a country other than the one in which the organization has its headquarters *or* an individual who manages an international or regional organization or a unit within it. Often, this manager is from the country where the organization's headquarters is located, but that need not be the case. The international manager is generally not a citizen of the country in which he or she is managing an overseas operation.

Overseas operation: An organization that is foreign to the country in which it is located. An overseas operation might be a field unit of an organization headquartered in another country or it might be an international or regional organization.

Home country: The country in which the organization has its headquarters.

Host country: The country in which the overseas operation is located.

Expatriate staff: Staff members at any level who are not from the host country and who have been assigned and transferred to that country by the organization's headquarters. We use this term broadly to include citizens of the home country and citizens of third countries whom the organization has assigned and transferred to the overseas operation. This latter type of employee is sometimes called a third-country national (TCN); also, some organizations refer to their expatriate staff as international staff. The principal distinction is that these employees are not citizens of the host country, which has implications with regard to their compensation and benefits packages, as well as their legal status in the host country and their familiarity with the local culture and norms.

Host country national (HCN): An employee of the overseas operation who is a citizen of the host country.

Looking Ahead

Having established that international management is different, with its own unique challenges and rewards, and that it is a growing field, let's take a quick look at the topics we will explore in the chapters that follow.

We have organized each chapter as an office call on one or both of the authors to discuss some aspect of international management. The table of contents is your schedule for a very busy day of consultations.

At "8:00 a.m.," you will meet with Ambassador Nagy (Tibor) to discuss the things that you, the international manager, need to do to prepare for and embark on your assignment. These will include consultations with people at headquarters and elsewhere, functional training, language and cultural training and even preparing your family members for a major change in their lives. Then we will fast-forward to your first few days at your overseas office and the things you will need to do to make a positive impression, embrace and be embraced by your new organization, and manage the expectations of those who work for you.

You will continue with Tibor at 8:45 a.m. to explore what it takes to be an effective leader in a global environment. Some of these factors are applicable to domestic as well as foreign assignments, but Tibor will argue that certain factors – especially keeping one's sense of humor and being highly attuned to one's surroundings -- are particularly critical when leading and managing overseas, where all eyes are upon you, even outside the office, and uncertainty is high.

In your meeting with Ambassador Engle (Greg) at 9:30 a.m., you will confront the elephant in the room: the fact that people from different cultures are indeed, in many important respects, different. Ironically, perhaps, we will explore cross-cultural relations by first looking at what people from different cultures actually have in common. One thing they have in common is that even people *within* their respective cultures are very different, so it is important for the international manager to avoid stereotyping and to develop a keen sense as to whether he or she is dealing with a cultural or an individual situation. Understanding the local culture is critical to developing this sense. Cross-cultural factors will underlie just about everything you engage in as an international manager.

One of the biggest differences between domestic and international management concerns human resources, and your meetings with us from 10:15 a.m. through 12:00 p.m. are devoted to this important topic. Naturally, when people from different countries work together in the same organization, cross-cultural factors come into play. But beyond these factors, there are practical concerns. How do you determine which positions should be filled by expatriate staff and which by host country nationals? Is there a need to hire third-country national employees with specialized skills or knowledge? Do you compensate all three types of employees according to the same plan? Is there information to which only one group has access (e.g., classified or proprietary information)? Does the staff work as an integrated team, or are there tensions between the

9

expatriates, HCNs and TCNs? Can your organization offer HCNs salaries and benefits that enable you to attract and retain top-flight talent on the local economy? Why does it seem that certain members of the expatriate staff constantly carp about their lifestyle, even though the overseas operation is providing them things -- such as housing, schooling for their children, recreational facilities and vacations – that they would have to take care of on their own if they were back at headquarters? These issues are the daily ration of the international manager, whether that individual is directly responsible for human resources management for the overseas operation or simply manages employees within his or her own unit. The head of an overseas operation, in particular, will want to be especially attuned to these unique human resource issues.

At 12:00 p.m., you'll join Tibor for a working lunch (we're tough, but not inhumane) to discuss the value, challenges and inevitable surprises of entertaining contacts in your host country. Business breakfasts, lunches, dinners and receptions can be extremely useful to advancing the objectives of your overseas operation and resolving some of the bureaucratic obstacles that you encounter vis-à-vis the host country government and other entities, but to be effective, you need to know the local rules governing hospitality and entertainment.

You will continue with Tibor at 1:00 p.m. to hear his thoughts on the many challenges the local environment poses to the overseas operation: different monetary units and exchange rate fluctuations that can destroy your best laid plans; the varying quality and reliability of local utilities and service (e.g., electricity, water, telephone service, etc.); harsh climatic conditions and their effect on sensitive computer equipment and other property; the lack of technical support for specialized equipment; and the host government's regulatory regime and the extent to which local officials observe it. And the list goes on. The extent to which such factors affect your overseas operation varies wildly from country to country. In some countries with generally reliable services and systems in place, differences in how one does business might only present the occasional irritant. In other countries, where nothing seems to work, at least in ways you would recognize as reasonably coherent, every day is a new dawn! Tibor will alert you to where some of these challenges might lie and offer suggestions as to how you can deal with them.

The leader and manager at home and abroad must rely on a wide range of contacts to achieve the organization's goals and objectives. The complexity of developing these contacts increases when you are managing an overseas operation, so at 1:45 p.m., you will meet with Greg to look at the international manager's universe of key relationships. These include officials at headquarters, of course, but also important contacts in the host country government and the commercial sector (regardless of the type of overseas operation one is managing), the local media, and even the diplomatic corps, which can offer the manager some unique insights and support. The head of an overseas operation and his or her senior team have to be out there getting to know people, understanding how they think, and enlisting their support in pursuit of the organization's objectives. It is not something that simply happens; it requires a sound and thoughtful strategy and a well-developed knowledge of the host country, its culture and its institutions.

At 2:30 p.m., Tibor will address a topic that the international manager of the 21st century would not dare neglect: the safety and security of his or her organization's personnel, property and resources, and in some cases, information. Globalization, in addition to bringing people in all corners of the world i-Pods and the Internet, has also ushered in transnational terrorism and often mounting crime. While some countries are safer than others, no country is safe in the absolute sense. Violent crime is sky-high in many countries, and foreigners, very often quite wealthy by local standards, are sometimes more likely to become its victims. Living in a place for a long time, one becomes savvy to its ways and develops an almost innate understanding of how to avoid potentially dangerous situations and how to behave if confronted with one. Much of that innate knowledge doesn't make the trip with you when you move overseas; you have to "relearn the ropes," to some degree. And if you are a newly arrived manager of an overseas operation, your own safety and security is only part of the problem: you will be responsible for many other people in this new environment whose threats and dangers you do not yet know. If you and other members of your expatriate staff have family members with you in the host country, the stakes are even higher. Tibor will

11

highlight many of the safety and security issues the international manager must be aware of and provide some guidance as to addressing them.

During your meeting with Greg at 3:15 p.m., we will look at crisis management overseas. Crises could span the range from natural disasters, like the Asian tsunami of 2004, to political events (e.g., coups, riots, military action), to airplane crashes and other manmade disasters that might cause mass casualties and threaten your organization and its people. Each country is different, of course, presenting its own potential crises and challenges in dealing with them. In more than a few countries, the international manager can reasonably assume that the host government and its security forces either will not or cannot offer much support in responding to a crisis. The manager and his or her team must anticipate the most likely crises and establish plans for dealing with them. We will discuss some of the common features of emergency plans for overseas operations, as well as mechanisms these operations have in place to stay on top of evolving situations and ensure that everyone in the organization is clued in to what's going on and prepared to act accordingly.

At 4:00 p.m., your meeting with Greg will turn to a topic closely related to crisis that we call "extreme management." By this, we mean managing in war zones and other areas where danger levels are exceptionally high and security forces other than the host country's are present to protect overseas operations and their staffs. The most obvious cases at the time of this writing are Afghanistan and Iraq, where Greg spent 13 months managing the administrative platform of the U.S. Embassy in Baghdad and its four regional embassy offices. Peacekeeping and humanitarian relief operations often fit this description, as well. Sadly, such situations have increased in recent years, forcing the United Nations, the governments of the United States and other countries, and NGOs to develop the capacity to address them via specialized overseas operations that often function very differently than those we spend most of this book discussing. Though extreme management is still the exception rather than the rule (thankfully), it is worth taking a look at some of its unique features as this phenomenon has generated a high demand for international managers.

So these are the subjects we will discuss with you during this busy "day" of consultations. Our objective is simple: to help you become an effective manager of overseas operations. Not only will your value to your organization thereby increase, but you'll be riding the crest of a global wave of growing demand for people with international management skills. That is hardly hyperbole; the trend is very clear. And beyond any benefit that might accrue to you or your organization, if you are as open, empathetic, curious, culturally sensitive, respectful, and knowledgeable in the ways of your host country as effective international managers need to be, you will contribute to better international understanding and good will.

8:00 a.m.

Meeting with Ambassador Nagy
Hitting the Ground Running

We're going to Lusaka, Zambia; everyone
says it used to be nice.

---One of the authors to his wife
on receiving his first overseas assignment

Lusaka, Zambia: *My wife and I watched the departure sign at London's Gatwick airport over several hours as the destination "Lusaka" slowly reached the top; it was time for us to board. Never having set foot on the African continent, we were both excited and apprehensive. We almost expected that our aircraft would be a small two engine commuter plane – after all, how many people would actually be going to an exotic destination such as Lusaka? It was, of course, a large jet – full of well-dressed delegates travelling to the Commonwealth Summit, being hosted that year by Zambia. All was well until we started our landing. Instead of taking a slow, gradual descent, the pilot stayed at cruising altitude and then started to corkscrew down immediately above the airport. On landing we were met by our "sponsors", there to make sure that we settled in as smoothly as possible. I asked about the strange landing, and my colleague replied, "Oh,*

15

all the planes have to land like that since the airport is surrounded by insurgent camps; they like to practice their shooting by taking potshots at low flying aircraft!" My wife and I looked at each other meaningfully – did we really want this "adventure?"

Getting Ready to Go

So you have your assignment and you're experiencing excitement, anticipation, uncertainty, hesitation, exhilaration, dread, or any combination of these – perhaps even changing from one hour to the next. You can reduce much of the anxiety by preparing thoroughly for your upcoming posting, and being sure to address all aspects of your future professional and personal life. In my experience, inadequate advance preparation was the single greatest cause of both professional failure and personal/family "disasters." Yet the departing international manager is often placed under tremendous pressure to get to the posting as quickly as possible to fill a critical staffing gap, or to bring some unique professional expertise which is urgently needed, or for any number of other really great reasons (especially from the point of view of the overseas office). Your overseas operation will likely assure you that needed training, language instruction, or pre-departure orientation will be taken care of "later" -- once you arrive. Unfortunately, this almost never happens, because you will be immediately thrust into full-time work while trying to cope with a totally new environment. So, taking time for advance preparation is essential; resist all attempts to short-cut the process – both for your own, and your organization's well-being! Following is a step-by-step guide to the most essential preparations:

Pre-departure Consultations

Talk to people with insight into your host country, the city where you'll be posted, and the overseas operation in which you'll be working. In some organizations the consultation process is formalized; in others, it will be totally informal. No matter what your organization's process, the key is to get as much useful information as possible about your future working and living environment. While you may be totally focused on the professional environment you are going into, remember to solicit questions and concerns of all family members – no matter how trivial. If it's important to them, it will be important to you.

Seychelles Islands: My wife and I, along with our nine-month-old triplets arrived in Victoria, capital of the Seychelles, on a Saturday morning, exhausted after a two day journey from Washington. Our well-meaning sponsors took us to our cavernous house, and left us to "rest up" after assuring us that it was fully provisioned to keep us through the weekend. What we found was a filthy house that had been locked up for weeks prior to our arrival, and a bottle of wine and some cheese for our "welcome." But there were no sheets, no infant formula, not even a place for the babies to sleep. We were also expected to attend a social function that evening, and to leave the kids with someone who had never babysat triplets. We ended up fixing three pull-out drawers as baby beds, using towels for their covers – but it was an unmitigated disaster. If I had investigated ahead of time exactly what we would need immediately upon arrival, even the type of residence, and communicated those requirements with the post, our tour in the Seychelles would have started on a much more harmonious note. Unfortunately, the rough start made the entire first year difficult, as it took us months to address the issues which could have been fixed in advance.

In discussing your future host country, living environments, and operations before departure, try to maintain as much objectivity as possible, and not accept the "spin" and hyperbole you will no doubt be given. It is most important to arrive at your new post in as neutral a mindset as possible. My family and I have greatly enjoyed postings which we had been assured were the worst in the world (e.g., Guinea), and I have gotten tremendous productivity out of employees I had been told were "worthless." On the other hand, residences we were assured would be "magnificent" turned out to be unlivable, and I had to deal in various ways with a number of employees who were described in advance as "superstars" but were unsuitable to the task.

Take in as much information from various sources as possible, no matter how contradictory. One fact you will learn is the overall image your international office has at headquarters, and in this case perception is reality. Once you know this, you can already start your strategy to either change that perception or reinforce it.

Conakry, Guinea: In 1996, Conakry was the US diplomatic post which had the highest rate of personnel curtailments (i.e., employees leaving before they should have.) When I was named ambassador I made it my priority to change this. On arriving I improved day-to-day living conditions for our U.S. staff (e.g., assuring everyone had a working generator in a city where electricity was off at least 80 percent of the time); and focused the work on effecting positive change in Guinea through cooperation with the Guinean government and opposition, rather than just condemning them for what they did wrong. Given Guinea's uncertain political stability, I also instituted regular open meetings for the entire American citizen community, so all Americans in country would know the latest developments. Within two years, Conakry changed from one of our lowest morale posts, to one with the highest rate for employees extending their tours of assignment.

If I had not fully investigated in advance all facets related to Guinea, the conditions of living in Conakry, and the working environment within the embassy, my tour would have been a disaster instead of a success.

Preparatory Functional Training

The time to learn your future job functions is *before*, not after arriving at your new post – especially if you are going to a small operation where you will be the only one doing certain types of work. While larger organizations usually have formal training programs to prepare their employees for their job functions, working in a smaller operation may be more complex and varied, requiring a wide scope of professional expertise. My most challenging work ever was in our five person embassy in the Seychelles Islands where I served concurrently as deputy to the ambassador, budget and fiscal officer, personnel officer, public affairs officer, security officer, housing officer, supply and transportation officer, political officer, economic officer, and commercial officer! Since most overseas operations are continuously undergoing personnel turnovers or absences due to other reasons, you should again be wary if you are told to "not worry" about preparatory functional training – because you will be provided with that after arrival. Chances are you will be expected to perform at full competence from the day you arrive, and you will be curtly asked, "Why didn't you learn that at headquarters before coming here?", if you profess a lack of knowledge about a job function. It will be especially critical to learn those functions which are covered by law or regulation, since your ability to quickly locate the correct operating procedures is inversely proportional to the priority of the task at hand. Over a weekend in Lomé, Togo, while holding down the fort with everyone else at an out of country conference, I had to figure out how to formally discharge a seaman from an American flagged vessel – never having even known that such a function was a U.S. Embassy responsibility until the U.S. Marine guard called to tell me a very anguished sea captain was at the gate.

Language and Cultural Training

Gone are the days characterized by the old joke: "What do you call someone who speaks three languages? (Trilingual) What do you call someone who speaks two languages? (Bilingual) And what do you call someone who speaks one language? (American!) Learn as much of the language of your new post as possible before departure. Of equal importance, try and arrange for your spouse and other accompanying family members to do the same. You may be operating in a working environment where the lingua franca will be English, but your spouse will likely have more day-to-day exchanges requiring direct communication in the local language; and those exchanges may impact whether you'll be dining on beef or bat that evening.

> **Lomé, Togo:** *Our ambassador's wife brought dinner conversation to a deadly silence by proudly announcing to the assembled that the soup contained no preservatives – that being the French word for "condoms." The dinner guests immediately proceeded to carefully examine the contents of their soup bowls, and the menu was not a hit.*

Aside from a small core of Anglophone countries, nations whose official language is English are composed of a variety of ethnic groups whose first language is something else. And please don't ever refer to a language as "tribal" or a "dialect" – Hausa in West Africa is spoken by more people than German is, worldwide. This also applies to countries whose official language is that of the former colonial power. In such cases, you should learn at least the most important phrases in the language spoken first by local people. It makes a huge difference in activities such as shopping, or ceremonial functions if you happen to know a few words of the "real" local language.

Yaounde, Cameroon: *When I served as deputy ambassador in Cameroon, every January 1 the diplomatic corps called as a group on President Biya to formally express their "best wishes" for the New Year. Each country's representative would go up individually to the President to shake hands and exchange courtesies. Cameroon was officially a French speaking country, so my colleagues all wished Biya "meilleures veux." From a Peace Corps volunteer I had learned how to say it in*

Biya's native Bulu; I was the only one to give my wishes for a good year to the President in his own language. His reaction was immediate, overwhelming, and totally delighted – and my colleagues were chagrined and envious! A small gesture, but with highly positive results.

Knowing something about the host country's culture is just as important as language capability. While you may be forgiven your linguistic inadequacies (Americans, generically, have set a low bar for you to overcome) a serious cultural faux pas can cause deep seated, long term damage. While there will likely be too many cultural "rules" for you to learn them all, you absolutely need to grasp the overriding features of your host culture, such as: sense of time; sense of personal space; touch or not to touch, and what parts of the body; length and form of greetings; gifts; topics which should or should not be raised; appropriate and taboo gestures or postures; appropriate and taboo colors; appropriate and taboo pets; appropriate and taboo clothing; English phrases or words which might sound like locally taboo words; and the list goes on....

Conakry, Guinea: *I felt sorry for my Japanese colleague and his wife: they meant well, yet often offended, and rarely really understood the Guineans. We did a joint US/Japan development project – he furnished the funding for a new village school, and I furnished a Peace Corps volunteer to supervise construction. When the building was finished, we held a lavish joint opening ceremony with all the villagers, the media, Guinean officials, and lots of speeches. With one innocent gesture, he and his wife turned what should have been positive publicity into resentment of Japan. His wife made the mistake of wearing dress gloves for the occasion – making all the Guineans believe she did so to avoid direct contact when shaking the many villagers' hands. On another occasion my Japanese colleague was beyond frustrated. The Guinean development minister had asked that Japan supply $100 million in development assistance, to which*

22

the ambassador replied, "We will consider it." The Guineans then enthusiastically announced that Japan would be furnishing Guinea an extra $100 million. The exasperated ambassador told me "when a Japanese says 'we will consider it' not only does it mean 'no,' but 'hell no!'" While my Japanese colleague had good language skills, he missed out on the equally important cultural communication.

Preparing the Family

While taking family along on an assignment serves as a source of tremendous support in trying to achieve "normalcy" in an alien environment, it also adds extra stress as lines between personal pressures and professional pressures tend to blur overseas. And I use the term "family" in the broadest possible sense – it can range from spouse, to significant other, to elderly parents, to a variety of minors, to pets and other combinations. The larger the group going the more complex the interpersonal dynamics, with each additional member (or pet) introducing even more attributes to be impacted by the new environment. As with your professional skills, I can't emphasize enough how critically important it is to prepare all accompanying family members for the "adventure." Again, larger organizations may have transition offices which specialize in providing post specific orientation. Smaller organizations without transition offices, or an individual moving overseas, still have access to tremendous resources on the internet, e.g., Department of State "Post Reports". Following are some of the more critical areas about which the family needs as much information as possible before the move:

- housing
- health conditions and medical resources
- educational facilities
- housing types, cost, availability
- safety/security/crime environment
- social environment for couples, singles, teens, children, alternative lifestyles, etc.

- availability of religious services

- availability of goods and services (and their cost)

- availability of car parts and repair services

- acceptance of credit cards (or wisdom in using them – e.g., never, ever use one in Nigeria!)

- availability of recreation

- availability of alcoholic beverages

- employment customs with domestic employees (maids, cooks, gardeners, babysitters, tutors, etc.)

The more information you and your family can obtain prior to departure, the fewer the unpleasant surprises and more realistic everyone's expectations. Under no circumstances should you try and present your new post through rose-colored glasses; the reality will soon become apparent and the reactions will be much worse than if expectations had been more realistic. Conversely, don't over focus on the negative – even Lagos and Djibouti have their attractions!

> **Lusaka, Zambia:** *By 1980 Zambia was broke and the country wasn't importing anything. One day we walked into Kabulanga, the "best" supermarket in Lusaka, and were delighted to find the shelves full. Until, that is, we realized that the only thing in the market was North Korean "strawberry" jam – not that there were any strawberries in the jars, just colored water and pectin, as far as we could tell. What made this more tolerable than tragic for us was that we had been well warned prior to coming to post, and had brought along a two year supply of basic consumables. Those folks who hadn't done their research ended up consuming many jars of the "jam."*

Hitting the Ground Running

The first few days at a new international office are critically important for putting the right imprint on your entire tour. When I co-chaired the training class the State Department conducts for new ambassadors, I put special emphasis on how to succeed in making that positive first impression. This book is meant to be useful to a greater variety of international executives than U.S. ambassadors, as each of you will be managing an international operation consisting of a multinational staff (home country, host country, and possibly third-country nationals) – so the same principles apply. Following is my recommended checklist for what to do upon arrival:

Plan your day/time of arrival. I tried to get to post when it would be the least inconvenient for my staff, and when I (and my family) would have an opportunity to rest before having to plunge into work, school or social interactions. No one is at their best after just finishing a long airplane trip and the stresses of departure. I found arriving the first weekend day seemed to work best, after first confirming the workweek at post -- i.e., some Islamic countries work Sunday-Thursday, etc. That way, only one or a small group of your new staff need to come to the airport, and you can use the weekend to rest, get your grounding, see some sights, stock up on necessities, show your children their new school, and be prepared for the workweek.

Staff taskings before arrival. There are several tasks you can assign to your new staff shortly before you arrive at post. This is both a useful exercise and a way to gage your new staff's responsiveness and efficiency. I would ask for the following things to be arranged ahead of time (obviously these depend on the size of the operation):

- A loose-leaf binder divided into organizational units with one page per employee including their photo, professional duties and personal/family info. This enabled me to match names and faces quickly.

- A reception I, with my family, would host for the organization "family" within the first week after arrival. The organizational size would help determine whether to

25

include all employees and adult family members, or just employees, or just key employees, etc. Being an embassy, for my first function I only hosted U.S. citizens – and a day later I met with the host country nationals. Most organizations could combine all nationalities to reinforce unity. At the reception I gave a "full disclosure" of my personal quirks (meetings are few, start on time and end quickly; I care about results not process, so staying at the office on weekends just to be seen doesn't impress me; family priorities come first; etc.) I also gave (briefly) my overriding goals and priorities for the operation, and thanked them for their accomplishments, dedication, and hard work. If you move directly into official quarters and they are large enough, it's great to hold the reception there since it sends the signal that the "captain is on board." If not, any site will do – however, I would not have the reception hosted by your deputy at her/his residence, as it is important to send the signal that this is your reception

Day 1 – Tour your new facility. It's important for as many of your new employees as possible to see you early on, and this gives you a chance to take a quick look at your operation with a fresh set of eyes Don't miss this opportunity – it will quickly pass. You can also observe the non-verbal dynamics among the staff – and see whether the first line supervisors know the names of all their employees, and can pronounce them correctly, etc. I delighted in visiting facilities – like the embassy warehouse or motor pool garage – which no ambassador had ever seen. You can be assured that rumors about you are already flying, so it's fun to try and make the rounds before the rumors do.

Day 1 – Meet the senior members of the team. I liked doing first a small group meeting, and later one-on-one sessions spread over a longer period. The group meeting is advantageous because everyone hears the same thing, and no one has a chance to "spin" news about the new boss to meet their own agendas.

Day 1 – Meet the host-country staff. If there is a clear division between home-country and host-country staff, it's critically important that you meet with the host-country group as quickly as possible to avoid raising (or reinforcing) any "us" vs. "them" perceptions. In some organizations the various nationalities are fully integrated with no differences among professional, skill, and salary levels – so this is not an issue. With other organizations, however, home-country nationals may occupy the top rungs while host-country nationals are the lower paid service employees and technicians. In any case, it is critically important for you to express as quickly as possible your support and appreciation for everyone under the organization's umbrella. Here again, I found that even using a few phrases of the local language made an enormous impact on the host-country staff. (So much so, that the day after I met with the Ethiopian staff, when I called on the Foreign Minister, he had already heard that the new ambassador "spoke Amharic.")

First Week – External calls. In diplomacy we use the term "calls" for initial official meetings outside the embassy to get to know our new colleagues, host country officials, business leaders, community leaders, religious leaders, etc., as appropriate to the specific post. Every organization has a set of key contacts and counterparts you need to meet as quickly as possible. I tried to find out before getting to post the handful of key people who I would have to meet quickly, and I asked the post to set up the meetings before I arrived. These were not necessarily those whom protocol would dictate that I meet with first, but rather those who would be the most useful contacts professionally to allow me to figure out what was really going on in the country, in my operation, etc. That way, my administrative assistant could intersperse my "have to" meetings (Foreign Minister, head of State Protocol, fellow ambassadors) with contacts who may not be high rank-wise, but would prove invaluable during my tour.

First Week – Host national employee union or professional association. If host national employees are represented by any association or union, I suggest meeting them the first week. They will likely present you with a list (usually years old) of accumulated issues they want you to deal with "immediately." I always found these meetings highly useful, both to get a sense of any "skeletons" lurking in the closet, and to project the points I

27

wanted to circulate within the organization. You should be prepared that one of the issues usually raised by the local association is a "long-overdue" across the board wage increase.

First Few Weeks – One-on-ones. Again, depending on the size of the operation, I tried to have one-on-one meetings with either the key employees, or, in smaller places, with all employees, within the first few weeks. I found the employees were tremendously flattered and quite forthcoming in discussing their goals, frustrations, suggestions for improving operations, etc. I also found almost universally that no one had ever done this with them before. Recognizing all the pressures on your time when you first get to post, I nevertheless urge you to do this, since the benefits are enormous, and the opportunity will pass quickly.

Managing Expectations

Your major goal during this segment of your process is to prepare thoroughly for your assignment and, once at your new international office, to create the impression you wish to project during the duration of your time at the post, and to establish the priorities you wish the international operation to follow now that you are in charge. By preparing in advance the core message you want to send on your arrival, and being consistent in what you say to each group with which you meet (of course there may be a certain 'spin' specific to each), you can make sure that the expectations you raise with your arrival are realistic, and in line with your own goals and management style.

Final Thoughts

A few additional rules which I found helped reduce stress during the transition from my predecessor:

- Don't badmouth your predecessor, immaterial of whether s/he was a success or failure. Your new staff undoubtedly holds widely varying views about her/him, so "exorcise" the ghost through your actions, not criticism.

- Do your best to avoid wide use of "when I was at (fill in your last post) we did this a different way and it worked much better." What you say may be true, but there are better ways of changing operating procedures than by constantly comparing your new operation to your previous one.

Meeting with Ambassador Nagy
                    Leading in a Global Environment

Don't just sit in your office and issue orders; go out and check for yourself. They will tell you what you want to hear – even if they know you are asking the impossible; they will say "yes" because you are the "big boss." If someone gives you an estimated time of completion, double it, then add 150 percent and maybe it will be done by then. Good luck – your predecessor never understood.

---Senior Zambian employee to one of the authors on his first day in Lusaka

Lusaka, Zambia: *During my first overseas management "opportunity" I served as the embassy "General Services Officer" in Lusaka. I was in charge of a mostly Zambian staff consisting of some white collar (accountants, inventory clerks) but mostly blue collar employees (drivers, plumbers, electricians, residential domestics). One day shortly after my arrival, the ambassador's wife called me in a panic because some of her valuable silver table service was missing and she expected me to find out who took it. While I had an excellent range of suspects – the ambassador's Residence staff – I had no idea how to proceed: should I question them myself; turn it over to the embassy security officer; ask the local police to intervene? One of my more senior Zambian employees told me not to*

31

worry, that he'd take care of it. The next morning the ambassador called to thank me for getting the silver back and to congratulate me on my 'brilliance.' Not having a clue what he was talking about, I asked my employee what he had done. To my amazement he had paid a marabou (aka witchdoctor) to meet with all of the residence staff and tell them that if the silver wasn't immediately returned, whoever took it, and their family, would be cursed with an incurable illness. End of problem and no more thefts during the ambassador's tenure. It certainly wasn't a leadership solution taught in George Washington University's master's program!

In this meeting we don't want to discuss leadership per se – we assume you already have a well-developed leadership style and don't need pointers on those fundamentals. Instead, we'll be focusing on types of issues you may never face in your home office, but which can take on major importance in an international setting. Whether you're directing a small one-of-a-kind non-governmental organization (NGO), or a regional corporate headquarters for a major global enterprise, there are unique challenges to leading in an international environment. For example, at home, leadership usually ends at the office door – as everyone goes home to a personal life which only occasionally intersects with work. In an international setting, however, your role extends way beyond the work environment and you may have to exercise leadership in a range of milieus, some of which may be way outside your comfort zone. Your community's expectations are high, and in certain environments -- especially hardship posts or those encountering a crisis - you will be the single biggest factor on the morale of your employees and their families, 24/7. And this, of course, can determine your success or failure, and that of your operation. Like it or not, you may be called on to serve as mayor, coach, family crisis counselor, priest, law enforcement officer, confessor, judge and jury. The following sections will cover some basic issues which are universal to all international operations.

Autocrat or Comrade – Finding the Right Balance.

Between the two of us, we served as deputies to ten ambassadors, who varied greatly in leadership styles, effectiveness, skills and intelligence. One challenge each faced, as do all chiefs of an overseas operation, is finding the right balance between being the "boss" while also being a member of your American community, facing the same hardships and challenges as everyone else living in that locale. While you may have certain privileges, like a dedicated car with driver, a much nicer residence, etc., you will share the general characteristics of your environment with your colleagues whether it's awful pollution, rampant crime, drug resistant malaria, 140 inches of rain, etc. In addition, you will likely interact with your subordinates and their families outside the office to a much greater extent than you would at home. We have found that the smaller the operation or the post, the greater the overall interaction. You work together, play softball together, have drinks at the American club or Marine House together, take weekend trips together, share holidays together, attend American School board meetings together, shop at the commissary together, etc. In certain small or isolated postings, you will feel like you are always together. And yet it really is important for the "chief" to maintain a certain level of separation from everyone else. This is especially tricky since overdoing it on either extreme will lessen your effectiveness as a leader. Elevate yourself too high, and you'll take on royal trappings earning ridicule or fear (both poison to your operation). Blur all distinctions, and you risk becoming indistinguishable from your subordinates and perhaps lose organizational control and discipline. In the following vignette, one of the ambassadors I served as deputy exhibited too much blue blood, almost in the vein of "let them eat cake!"

__West Africa:__ Overseas, especially in hardship environments, items we take for granted in the U.S. can be rare delicacies. In one African post I served as deputy to an ambassador who, while basically a very nice person, was totally clueless about some of the day-to-day hardships the rest of the staff had to endure. It was a city

33

with high crime, terrible weather, spotty electricity and water, abysmal health conditions, and chronic shortages of most basic commodities. For Thanksgiving, our very small commissary had pre-ordered long in advance (since shipments could take weeks) enough turkeys for each family at post, since turkeys were unavailable locally. The week before Thanksgiving, our ambassador's spouse decided that she would organize a traditional American Thanksgiving meal for local dignitaries, and bought all of the turkeys from the commissary. The local national commissary manager was too intimated by her position to refuse. To avoid an out and out mutiny by the embassy staff I had to explain to our ambassador the significance of his wife's actions and the devastating effect it had on post morale, and frankly, the negative consequences for him if some employees decided to curtail their tours because of such insensitivity. Reluctantly the ambassador asked his wife to return the extra turkeys and some of the damage was undone – but he lost the staff's respect and dedication and subsequently received a scathing report when the post was inspected.

Complicating the equation is the expected office protocol of the locale – which can range from the stilted formality of Switzerland to the super casual Seychelles, where ties are forbidden by presidential decree. Your local employees will also expect a certain leadership style based on their culture: be too informal in an autocratic system and lose their respect; be overly formal in a casual environment and risk ridicule. We'll have more comments on cultural issues in the next meeting. In any case, do consider these factors in deciding where you will come out on the scale ahead of time – while you can certainly make minor adjustments once you arrive, it will be difficult to insist that everyone address you as "Mr. Director" after you already told them to call you "Fred" when you landed at the airport. But formality does need to be situational.

Victoria, Seychelles: Our entire embassy staff of six was assembled on the tarmac at Victoria Airport waiting for the arrival of our new ambassador. The prior one had left a few weeks back to the relief of all of us. He had taken himself, and the role of our very insignificant country in the overall scheme of U.S. Geopolitics, way too seriously. We maintained strict schedules and formal office procedures in the most casual and relaxed country on earth, where the only folks who suffered heart attacks were the tourists; it was totally ridiculous! We had bombarded Washington with reports no one read on issues no one cared about, and we were hoping for a change with the new leadership. When the plane arrived our new ambassador was the first one out, and when I greeted him with "Welcome Mr. Ambassador," the first words out of his mouth were: "Call me David!" What a wonderful change – not only in tone – but in substance. Almost immediately the office environment became more relaxed, and we began focusing on real priorities – not trying to duplicate the work of a large embassy, but on what was really important for where we were, e.g., finding out about Soviet ship visits and increasing U.S.

influence, over beers on the beach! Morale and productivity both skyrocketed.

You're There – Now What?

In the previous meeting we discussed ways to "hit the ground running." Now you have arrived and are settling in, assuming responsibility for an operation which will likely involve multiple cultures, languages, ethnicities, and regulations, in an environment which will give you and your American colleagues varying degrees of culture shock. Again, cultural issues are covered in the next meeting – but suffice to say here, sometimes postings in places with the most similarities to the U.S. are the most difficult, because Americans tend to have a high expectation for what they consider "normalcy." You do have to realize from day one, that you are in charge of four very different constituencies, often with competing interests:

- Your fellow American expatriates, posted temporarily from the U.S., just like you.

- Host country national employees, many of whom spend their entire careers with your organization in their country; they see many sets of Americans come and go during their tenure.

- Third country nationals (TCNs) who either reside in the country, or are brought in by your company -- temporarily or long term -- because of their expertise. Some organizations treat U.S. residents of the country as TCNs, others as if they were hired from the U.S.

- Family members accompanying your American employees on assignment from the U.S.

While future meetings will cover the specifics of human resources management in greater detail, what we'd like to highlight here is that you will have to meld your own leadership style with the cultural expectations of your locale, the cultural realities of the groups of people you are managing, the culture of your organization, conditions of local life (i.e. is the kidnap threat so great that you cannot reasonably expect people to work after dark?), and expectations of your American community.   Not easy, but not impossible.

"All in the Family"

While the cultures of your various constituencies may differ, along with their salaries, work regulations and benefits, we found the most important thing is for you as the leader to instill a sense of "family" among them all.   Following are some suggestions:

Communicate with everyone.   Some information is essential to give to everyone at the same time, other information is to be shared with only certain groups or individuals (the "need to know" principle), but ALL must feel like they are being included in the communication chain.

> *Addis Ababa, Ethiopia: Managing our embassy in Ethiopia in the late 90s was a challenge. The Ethiopian government was very unhappy with the U.S., so our Ethiopian employees --- many of whom had worked for us for decades – were feeling much divided loyalties.   The resident American community, most of which disagreed with official U.S. policy towards Ethiopia, was downright hostile. And our official American community was feeling under siege.   I decided the best course of action was to communicate with all groups as often as possible and to try and find venues for all three to mix. In addition to weekly "country team" meetings for select U.S. staff, I initiated monthly open 'CT' meetings for all U.S. employees and their adult family members. I also started meeting regularly with our Ethiopian employees through an interpreter, where I carefully explained why U.S. policy was the way it was, how much I appreciated their working for us under difficult circumstances, and that I understood that their first loyalty had to be to their own country. I also inaugurated monthly "town hall" meetings for all American citizens in country, where I again explained U.S. policy and shared whatever information I*

could about safety and security. At all meetings I responded to questions and concerns. We also organized a joint awards ceremony for all embassy employees, with Ethiopian and American food and remarks in English with interpretation. For American holidays, we organized special programs for the entire community so, for example, the children of American missionaries, our Ethiopian co-workers, and our U.S. diplomats all did "trick or treating" together at American residences. After several months, everyone did start feeling as members of one family, and morale and productivity all improved markedly.

What's really going on here?

Based on their previous experience, the host national staff may look at you as yet another clueless American who they will have to endure for a few years before you move on, to be replaced by someone much like you – in an ever-repeating cycle. Many overseas operations are run by the local employees with American supervisors who are reluctant to actively manage – having assumed that the principle, "if it isn't broken, don't fix it" applies. This is usually a mistake.

__Lusaka, Zambia:__ My first time managing overseas was in Zambia in 1978, and I was quite naïve in believing that the word "ethics" meant the same thing everywhere. Although I was nominally in charge of all embassy contracting, I totally trusted my local purchasing assistant, who dutifully went out daily to buy a wide variety of goods. I carefully reconciled the receipts weekly, and ascertained that we did receive the goods and that the prices were reasonable. About a year later, I hired a Tunisian-American, the spouse of an embassy employee, as my assistant. Coming from a totally different culture, he automatically assumed that there were scams going on in our operations, and he took a careful look at local purchasing. He found that our local purchasing assistant was buying most of his goods from a single source and that the receipts were sequential – i.e., the embassy seemed to be the company's only *customer. On further investigation he found that this company was owned by our purchasing assistant's cousin, and that we were routinely paying twenty to thirty percent higher than what the goods were generally priced. From that point on, I became much more careful about scams, and continuously uncovered a series of attempts to defraud our embassy wherever I served. We'll discuss some of these things in a later meeting.*

Ethnic politics. Outside of being a dual national of the country where you are posted, just accept that you will never fully understand the local culture or ethnic dynamics. Despite this handicap, you can still lead effectively by learning some of the major cultural aspects and incorporating them into your managing. For example, in Sub-Saharan Africa, European colonizers created artificial states without regard to history, geography, or ethnic composition. As a result, an operation employing local nationals will likely have an ethnic mix of groups distrustful, or openly hostile towards each other. Or, because the local HR manager is from one ethnic group, that group may be totally over-represented among the local staff. Both situations need careful attention.

Yaounde, Cameroon: Linguistically, Cameroon is much like Canada, except with the language groups reversed: it's about twenty percent English speaking and eighty percent French. Additionally, the important northern area, although nominally Francophone, has a strong Islamic/Arabic influence. Although the government was dominated by Francophones and Northerners, almost all embassy employees were Anglophone – they were easier for the U.S. staff to deal with, and the local HR manager was one, so most local employees were from his area of the country. Despite strong resistance from the local staff, I acted quickly to change this – starting with the motor pool -- using the rationale that when our American diplomats traveled throughout the country, they should have drivers who know the local roads, language, customs, etc. At first the local HR manager claimed to be unable to find "qualified" applicants from other ethnic groups – but threatened with loss of his own job, he grudgingly relented. Eventually the differing ethnic groups started working together. By diversifying our local workforce, we also began receiving much better information about what was going on in various parts of the country, and how Cameroon's volatile ethnic mix was coexisting on any one day.

Working the real hierarchy. Every organization has an informal hierarchical structure as a companion to the company's formal version. In multi-ethnic environments there may be several informal versions, with each ethnic group's "pecking order" distinct from those of the others. Leading effectively means learning them all for your organization, so that you can use the informal structure when you have to make absolutely sure a message is communicated correctly and expeditiously throughout the organization, or some extraordinary issue needs careful handling. Greg and I have often consulted the senior member of an ethnic or linguistic group, to make sure a policy is fully understood, or to solicit advice on how to proceed on a sensitive subject in a culturally appropriate manner. This person may have a low formal standing in the organization -- like the 70 year old electrician who worked for me in Ethiopia -- but s/he is more respected and has much higher status in the eyes of the local staff than the American (or French) supervisor.

Setting uniform standards. Immaterial of culture or ethnicity, there are certain non-negotiable principals which, while perhaps not locally appropriate, nevertheless have to be followed. For example, there can be no compromise on certain U.S. standards for ethical behavior, such as complying with the Foreign Corrupt Practices Act, non-discrimination, sexual equality, private gain from company resources, etc. We have found that while it's often difficult to explain the rationale for such standards within the local context, once we make it absolutely clear that there is no flexibility, and the local staff understands that we mean it, there will be acceptance. In some regions, like Sub-Saharan African countries, office workers routinely take home office supplies. Others may take the tools of their trade for moonlighting during work hours, while housekeepers will take laundry soap, linens, etc. In such environments we explained carefully to new staff that unlike other enterprises, the embassy paid a much higher salary, but we expected work during work hours, and no pilfering. Sometimes we've had to establish our seriousness by discharging non-compliant employees, but that serves as an example for others. In locales with endemic corruption problems (like West Africa) you must remain vigilant throughout your tour, and you may fire one incumbent after another. One absolute rule – there can be no double standard for local and American staff; otherwise you will never be taken seriously again.

East Africa: *In one of my postings a senior American employee was flouting the regulations. He was paying his driver significant overtime for unofficial purposes, and he was smoking on U.S. government premises and in U.S. government owned vehicles despite regulations to the contrary. Everyone knew he was doing this, but no one*

thought anything would happen because of his position. In addition, I was also just weeks from departure, so the easy thing would have been to simply leave the issue for my successor. Reluctantly, I asked his agency to withdraw him from post, because I knew that his behavior was sending the message that there were different standards of behavior for different categories of employees. It was a battle, but I prevailed; his departure made a huge impact on U.S. and local employees, and morale improved significantly.

Dealing with problem employees. While the above illustrates an especially sensitive case, we were faced with having to deal with difficult employees at all of our postings. In some cases these were local employees – and we had to proceed delicately in compliance with local labor laws. In others, they were Americans assigned to post – and it sometimes seemed that the headquarters personnel office made it a rule to assign at least one person to each post whose job it was to make life miserable for everyone else. Sometimes it was a third country national, or an accompanying family member, which introduced another set of complexities. While we'll describe such situations in detail in a later meeting, the important point is that you need to take action with all deliberate speed. And your ultimate decision is whether you can deal with the issue at post (if it involves a non-resident employee), or you need to send the employee away. In our types of operations, there is a great temptation to await action – after all, you will be leaving eventually, or the problem person may be leaving, or the situation may change, and no one wants to disrupt a family in the midst of the school year, etc. We found too many of our colleagues in leadership positions took this easier route – which resulted not only in the entire operation suffering needlessly, but the problem being handed off to someone else, either at that post or at another. Ignoring problem employees helps neither them, nor their families, nor the organization. Just the fact that you are reading this book proves that you want to be an effective leader, so when you are confronted with a difficult personnel issue, act!

Giving your staff a life. As we said at the beginning of this session, leading an international operation means assuming responsibility for the welfare of your employees beyond work. Because of the inherent hardships of living in an international setting, families endure many more pressures than they do at home. For example, never knowing when the water or electricity would be on in Zambia made daily life hell with three newborn triplets who produced mountains of dirty diapers daily! The potential result of these hardships is that for occupations such as our diplomatic service, alcoholism, divorce, children's behavioral problems, and other similar conditions are higher than in the general population. You can make a major contribution to preventing such problems, and in general improving community morale by proactively discouraging workaholism. Here you set the tempo, and it's your culture that matters – not the country, not the company, not your employees. When you first arrive, your staff will be watching for clues as to your unstated expectations – we found that in this case (as with most) state what you want. Greg and I are both strong believers in balancing work priorities with life, and what matters is productivity, not time spent at the office being seen by the boss.

And finally – keep your sense of humor. You will be exasperated and befuddled and bewildered by questioning why certain things are done the way they are in Country X. Initially you may try and totally change your new locale to make it more like "America." It won't work. Paper towel dispensers will still be installed upside down by workers who have never used one; electrical cords in the workshop will still be lying in rain puddles; promised deliveries will not arrive when promised; and that wonderful phrase "any time from now" will still be used in response to any number of questions. In Lagos, Nigeria, probably the most dysfunctional environment either of us has known, there was a wonderful expression: WAWA (West Africa Wins Again)! At the time, it was a phrase used to describe terribly frustrating events. But even then we knew that in the future – if we lived that long – we would look back on those events and smile. In such situations your frustration and rage will only lead to health problems for you. Some of the most frustrated people in West Africa are Swiss diplomats and business representatives (and Northern Europeans in general) whose anally retentive lifestyle just cannot adapt to the local "laissez faire" rhythms. Such folks still show up for events scheduled for 5:00 p.m. at 5:00 p.m., while everyone else knows to come at 7:00 p.m.! Nigerians, on the other hand, despite unbelievable hardships of daily life, consistently poll as among the happiest people on Earth. The point is, a sense of humor will go a long way toward keeping you (and your employees) much healthier and much more productive. Even if the plane doesn't arrive or depart, the sun will still come up in the morning!

Addis Ababa, Ethiopia: We'll talk about "managing in a crisis" later – but being ambassador on September 11th, 2001 in Ethiopia transcended the term. When the planes hit the towers and the Pentagon, no one knew what was going on, or what else would happen. In Ethiopia, right next door to Somalia's anarchy and home-grown Islamist terrorists, our community felt especially vulnerable. Our embassy "family" needed the assurance that someone was clearly in charge, even if the overall situation seemed out of control. Our wider American citizen community was desperate for information, and the sense that someone was doing everything possible to keep them safe. And our Ethiopian "hosts" – both the government and ordinary citizens – were eager to show their concern and support, since their society had been victimized by terrorists for decades. I spoke with the Ethiopian leadership by phone within hours of the World Trade Center attacks – asking them to increase security for our facilities – including the American School – and known private American operations, such as companies and missionary organizations. The Prime Minister agreed and dispatched additional security personnel within hours. While we had to tighten access to the embassy, ordinary Ethiopians began coming with flowers. We received the bouquets graciously, and placed them at the foot of our flagpole – creating a mountain within three days. We met frequently with the embassy staff to provide as much information as we had, and organized several "town hall" meetings for

44

all American citizens so we could tell them everything we could. I went on Ethiopian TV the day after the attacks, to do a live, one hour, one-on-one interview to thank the Ethiopians for their concern and support, and to state clearly that Islam was not our enemy, terrorists were. My most difficult personal task, however, was organizing and conducting a memorial service for the American community several days after the events. We needed to bring everyone together to grieve and be reassured, and give our people a way to vent their anger and sadness. It was the most challenging venue I've ever presided over or spoken at, but under such circumstances the leader has no choice. Overall we did very well – our community emerged closer, stronger, and with a renewed dedication to our mission. As I said at the beginning of this session, managing in an international setting requires leaders to assume a variety of roles, whether or not they are comfortable with them.

Meeting with Ambassador Engle
                         Cross-Cultural Factors: Cracking the Code

Toto, I've a feeling we're not in Kansas anymore.
---Dorothy, "The Wizard of Oz"

Rural Togo: *As I arrived at a Togolese village to participate in an event, the district prefect (chief officer), the village headman and a line of village elders were there to greet me. After shaking many hands, I found myself, the prefect at my side, standing in front of two wizened old men, each no taller than five feet and both festooned with an array of feathers, animal fangs, pelts and other fetishes. These were the village's traditional healers, medicine men. One was holding a live chicken, the other a calabash of thick, milky liquid with a few flies floating on top. "Oh no, traditional beer," I thought. As I reached for the calabash, silently marveling at the extremes to which I was willing to go to serve my country, the prefect whispered, "No! It's not to drink!" (Thank you, Lord!) The old man holding the calabash proceeded to pour a circle of the milky gruel at my feet, after which he produced a knife, and the presence (and fate) of the chicken became clear. The old men partially slit the chicken's throat and squirted its blood into the circle. As the assembled villagers intently observed the ceremony,*

47

the prefect advised me, "This will determine if your visit is auspicious." The chicken had already reached its own conclusion.

Okay, you're going to work in another country, and being the sophisticated person that you are, you know very well that people there will be different. They will have different ways of thinking and behaving; perhaps they will speak a different language or even multiple languages; they might practice a different religion or have a very different ideological framework. You're prepared to be open to these differences and learn as much about them as you can, so that they don't catch you off guard as you assume direction of your operation and settle in as an eager new resident of your country of assignment. Great! Now you're anxious to jump right in and explore these differences, these so-called cross-cultural factors.

Whoa! Understanding cultural differences *is* absolutely vital to your success as an international manager. But there are a few things we need to address before exploring the factors that make another culture different, so that knowledge of these factors is built on a solid foundation.

First, understanding that people in other countries are different needs to be grounded in what I believe is an equally (if not more) important fact: People the world over are more alike than they are different from one another. They laugh and cry, very often in the same situations that make you and me laugh and cry. They are immensely concerned about the welfare of their families and take great pride in their children's accomplishments. They are deeply saddened by the loss of a loved one. They worry about their finances and are concerned about job security. They appreciate being treated with respect, and they believe it is important to be hospitable to a guest or visitor. Having the knowledge that individuals from different countries are more alike than they are different affords you a powerful tool in cross-cultural communication: empathy.

Addis Ababa, Ethiopia: *While I was serving as Management Counselor of the U.S. Embassy in Ethiopia, the dignified and beloved embassy driver who took our children to and from the international school died suddenly of an infection. Ato (Mr.) Fantaye had a special place in my family's heart, because he insisted on accompanying our shy and sometimes weeping daughter to her kindergarten class each day, standing by her until the teacher would finally send him out. At his funeral, my sadness led to tears, and I'm not normally one to cry. Later, one of the embassy's Ethiopian employees made a point of telling me how much it meant to the Ethiopian staff that I had attended the funeral and so openly and sincerely expressed my grief along with the rest of them.*

Now, my second, seemingly contradictory, point: People within your own culture have different personalities that affect their behavior and how they interact with other members of society. Although they might react in the same way under certain circumstances and share some beliefs that derive from the culture, you would never think of everyone in your country as being the same. So don't fall into that trap with regard to other countries. Like you, people in other societies share among themselves a set of customs, beliefs, values, habits and behaviors that collectively form their culture, but even as they are guided by these cultural factors, they can still be, and are,

49

different from one another as individuals. Every country has hardworking folks, lazy ones, jokers, people of somber demeanor, etc. But didn't we just say that people are more alike than they are different? Indeed, we did, and we stand by that assertion. The point here is that, to the extent that someone from another country is not like you, that difference might have a cultural basis or may simply be the result of your being unique individuals. To manage an overseas operation effectively, it's important to distinguish consistently and instinctively between cultural and individual (personality) differences and avoid the well-worn short cut of too many people who venture abroad: stereotyping.

Understanding and being sensitive to cross-cultural factors does *not* mean that you have to transform yourself into someone else, trying to become a member of the culture in which you are working and living. That would be nearly impossible. What's more, people in your country of assignment – especially those who work for you -- really won't expect that of you. They *will* greatly appreciate it if you make an effort to learn about their culture and customs and even take part in some of their cultural celebrations and activities. Such knowledge will help you to avoid unwittingly causing offense, and the more intimately your work requires you to be integrated into traditional communities, the more important this will be. Peace Corps Volunteers, for example, receive a lot of cross-cultural training because they very often live and work in villages and communities where few other foreigners have ever been. People in those communities are sometimes barely familiar with the notion of someone being foreign or from another culture. In such situations, the more one understands the local culture and can even observe certain of its practices, the better one will be accepted. That said, the local people are always going to view and treat the foreigner as just that: someone who is not like us. In my opinion, you should have as your objective to be a well-informed, aware and interested foreigner who values and respects cultural differences. Most of the time, trying to "go native" is just too weird.

Let's take that a step further. Everyone who lives abroad, whether as a diplomat or otherwise, is representing his or her own country. You really have little choice in this regard; this is simply how people perceive you. On the one hand, one hopes that a person in this situation doesn't represent the worst of the country he or she comes from. Implicit in the moniker "Ugly American" is someone doing just that. But every culture has its strong points: hospitality, generosity, industriousness, friendliness, open-mindedness, whatever they might be. Emphasizing these positive characteristics in your behavior without lecturing others about them – or about their absence in the host culture – is a great way to lead by example, especially if the characteristic you're trying to share will help the group better achieve its task.

__Hongcheon, South Korea:__ Thirty years ago, as a Peace Corps tuberculosis control volunteer in rural South Korea, I quietly bucked local culture in favor of the "American" way on a few occasions to get things done on behalf of the county health center. On one such occasion, our provincial x-ray truck got stuck in a sudden snowstorm as we were making our rural rounds. No one knew what to do, and we were out in the middle of nowhere. I asked the driver if he had any snow chains for his tires, to which he replied in the affirmative, admitting in the same breath that he didn't know how to put them on. My other colleagues claimed ignorance, as well. A veteran of innumerable Colorado snowstorms, I started to get down on my hands and knees to do the job, but the four or five Koreans around me protested: "Wait! You're an educated person. You mustn't do this dirty work." They were quite serious. My status and reputation were at stake. As the snow continued to pile up at our feet and my colleagues began to shiver more violently (since they had chosen not to wear winter coats in favor of fashion), I finally ignored their objections on behalf of my dignity, crawled under the truck, and put the chains on. On the way back to the health center, they had great fun teasing me about my new status as the local mechanic, but they were warm and happy, and I was featured as the hero of the story as it later made its rounds through the community.

There's always going to be some broken "cultural china," but the more you know about the local scene, the better you will be at avoiding such situations. You can thereby save your "sharp elbows" for times when you really need to use them on behalf of the organization or some other important cause. As a leader and manager, there will definitely be times when you must insist that things are done *your* way, whether that's consistent with the local culture or not. To navigate such situations effectively, it's important for you to know who you are and how your own culture shaped you, what the local culture would normally dictate under the circumstances, why that's not going to work, and how you intend to buck the system and deal with the blowback.

Common Cross-cultural Factors

Now that we've addressed *how* to think about cultural differences, let's look at some of the principal ways in which cultures differ. There are many books and theories on this subject, and I will not attempt to survey or even cite them here. What I present in this chapter is based for the most part on my own observations and those of Tibor, and our endless hours of conversation over more than a collective half-century with fellow travelers, gracious hosts and friends around the world. Those who have traveled abroad will readily recognize many of the factors I'll mention in the following paragraphs.

Language

When people in the country to which you are assigned speak a language other than the one you speak, this will generally be the most obvious difference between you and them. In your earlier meeting with Tibor, he touched upon the language issue in discussing preparations for a foreign assignment. Because differences of language can have such a great impact on your assignment and your effectiveness in directing an overseas operation, however, it's worth expanding on the topic.

English-speakers take comfort in the fact that English has increasingly become the language of international communication; the tourist and commercial trades in most common travel destinations take this into account. But relying on people in other countries to speak your language makes you vulnerable in a few critical respects:

- In large cities, and in organizations and businesses that typically deal with foreigners, you might find a sufficient number of people who speak your language, but up-country, and especially in more rural areas, you could be lucky to find someone who speaks anything but the local language. Then what?
- If the person with whom you wish to converse doesn't speak your language, you're either going to have to find someone who can interpret for you, or be reduced to very elementary communication.
- Even when you find someone who speaks your language, you might not be sure how well he or she understands it or what you're saying. Many people become very adept at faking comprehension, often to be polite. Do the words you and your interlocutor are using mean the same thing to both of you? If you're relying on others to speak your language, you're in their hands.

There's another very important way in which you'll be vulnerable not knowing the local language of the country to which you're assigned: You will be robbed of the rich cultural signals and information laced throughout the language. How a concept or a thought is expressed in a language tells you much about what's important to its native speakers. Culture shapes the language and language shapes the culture. A lot of information having to do with etiquette, manners, and social structure is encoded in the language. Several languages (German, French and Spanish, for instance) have formal and informal verb forms, and using the wrong one can cause great offence. In Korean, there are five such forms, one of which, directly translated as "half language," is only used to communicate with children and one's wife (but not one's husband). Don't use that one with the professional contacts you're trying to develop. All languages contain these culturally loaded words, structures and usages, so one key to cracking the code of the local cultural is very definitely knowledge of the language. For many of us, in fact, it's this cultural code cracking that makes learning another language so enjoyable and rewarding, despite the obvious challenges and the inevitable mistakes. (By the way, be courageous and speak the language openly and often as you learn it. It's the only way to become proficient. Don't sweat your mistakes.)

Social distance is yet another result of not knowing how to speak the local language. First, even if you struggle at it, people will appreciate your attempts to speak their language and adapt yourself to life in their country. Second, of course, if you speak the language, the number of people you can speak to directly will increase considerably. Your social network and the information it yields will expand dramatically.

Despite the very clear social and cultural advantages, the decision to invest time in learning the local language is a tough call. Becoming proficient in another language takes a lot of work and hours of study. You might find that in fact there are many speakers of your language in your country of assignment and that you are able to converse with your principal professional contacts quite well. English is so widely spoken by professionals, office workers and service industry personnel in Pakistan and India, for instance, that this might be the case. If you do in fact determine that you will not be able to get by in your own language, which language do you learn? In many countries, there are several language groups and none is necessarily dominant. This is certainly true in several African countries, although in many the former colonial language (English, French, Portuguese) is widely spoken and still used in official correspondence and records.

A word about using interpreters: Even if you speak the local language, in certain situations, such as negotiations or discussions with senior officials, it is often useful to engage an interpreter. If precise communication is important to the dialogue, using the interpreter allows you to worry about your message rather than the vocabulary and grammar of a foreign language. The time it takes the interpreter to translate and convey the message to either party in the conversation also affords you time to formulate your thoughts. If you speak the local language, using the interpreter gives you the opportunity to hear the message twice and ensure its accuracy. If, in fact, you don't speak the local language and you really must rely on an interpreter to convey your message accurately, you better know something about that person's loyalties and interpretation skills. Does the interpreter work for you or your interlocutor?

> ***Lomé, Togo:*** *When I was presenting my ambassadorial credentials to the president of Togo, a very formal and traditional ceremony and our first meeting, I told him in English that I looked forward to working with the members of his government. The president's official interpreter told him in French that I did not look forward to working with the members of his government. As the president's brow furrowed, one of my embassy counselors quickly corrected the interpreter and alleviated the president's concern that the United States had sent a disagreeable new ambassador to represent it in Togo.*

Religion

Differences of language can certainly affect intercultural communications and often require considerable effort to address. They are, however, not normally as value-laden and fraught with potential cross-cultural hazard as differences of religion. All of the world's major religions have their adherents in the United States, but many Americans rarely interact with people of other religions, especially in less urbanized areas. Even when they do, religion is generally off the radar screen of their interaction, given the secular nature of American society. In more traditional cultures, however, religion has much a greater effect on the ebb and flow of daily life, local politics, the economy, education, and other social institutions.

It is very important for someone managing an organization overseas to understand the influence of religion on local society and the culture. Some of the questions you will want to raise in this regard will be quite practical: When are the religious holidays? How are they observed? Do most businesses shut down, and are most employees generally given the day or days off? Does the dominant religion affect the calendar in other ways, such as the Thursday/Friday or Friday/Saturday weekend observed in the Muslim world? Are there times of day that have religious significance or require the observance of religious practices, such as the Muslims' five daily prayers? How do most local employers facilitate such practices?

Other aspects of a country's religious life might be more emotionally charged and have an equally direct effect on your organization: If there are multiple religions, do their members coexist peacefully or is there serious tension between them? Do adherents of the different religions work together in the office or on work teams constructively? Will the adherent of one religion work for or be supervised by the adherent of another? Does your own religion or aspects of its practice provoke any reaction from citizens of the host country? Does it affect your ability to supervise people from the host country or engage with key contacts outside your organization?

Then there are the more subtle factors: How intensely does religion affect the lives of people in the host country? How observant are they? How does their religion affect their notions of destiny, personal responsibility and will, authority, fairness, etc.? To what extent does the local religion(s) serve to hold in check crime, corruption, promiscuity, or sexually transmitted diseases?

As an international manager you are going to want the answers to all of these questions. In addition, you are going to want to inform yourself about the basic tenets of the principal religions which people in your country of assignment practice, and you'd be well served to establish good relations and productive contacts with influential members of the significant religious communities. The respect that you demonstrate for the country's religious communities will send signals to their adherents – those on your staff, those in important government positions, clergy and other influential members of these religious communities, and the local titans of commerce -- that you are a fair and sympathetic person, someone worthy of their respect.

> **Lomé, Togo:** *As ambassador to Togo, I regularly hosted events at which I would bring together religious leaders from all major local faiths, usually over a meal carefully prepared to meet the various dietary restrictions of their religions. Although inter-faith tension was not an issue in Togo, my guests always commented on the fact that it took the U.S. ambassador to bring them together to*

explore the role of religion in Togolese life. Each year I would also host an iftar dinner for Muslim leaders during Ramadan. I was prepared to have my guests perform their ritual ablutions (cleansing) beside my swimming pool, but I was unprepared, the first year, for the number of extra guests that my invited guests brought with them. The following year, food and places to sit were in abundance.

Concepts of Time

What does an American mean when he says he's going to do something "right now"? Can he safely assume that his South African friend means the same thing when she says she'll get to something "just now"? Will the proverbially punctual German be embarrassed arriving fifteen minutes late to a conference in Ghana? More likely, she'll be bored for the next hour and a half as she waits for the African participants to arrive.

People from different types of cultures have very different concepts of time. In industrialized, developed, largely urbanized countries – we'll refer to these as "modern" countries for the purposes of this exposition -- the 24-hour clock has come to rule our lives. Americans grow up with the injunction "Time is money." Most people in modern countries have their days mapped out in time slots, either mentally, or physically on their desk diaries: "This morning, I'm going to attend meeting X at 9:30 a.m. and meeting Y at 11:00 a.m. By noon, I need to accomplish A, B and C, then in the afternoon..." Time, in their world is linear – from this to this to this – and "manmade."

Imagine the African or Latin American villager's "desk diary" (which is probably the position of the sun or the weather): "Let's see, it's getting muggy; the rainy season will be here soon. (Days? Weeks? Certainly not by 3:00 p.m. this afternoon!) I need to plant my maize," which will occur in bits and pieces over the weeks that follow. In countries that are still primarily rural, or which are just becoming urbanized – we'll call these countries, societies or cultures "traditional" for the sake of this discussion -- the notion that human beings rather than nature decide what time it is can be a pretty foreign concept. As such, the behavior of people in more traditional societies often won't reflect the same "respect for time" (i.e., being a slave to a clock that's divided down to the second) that some from the modern world might expect. People from traditional cultures are not being rude or disrespectful when they show up late to a meeting or fail to get something done "on schedule." They are, virtually, marching to the beat of a different drummer, and one who's been around a lot longer than the one rapping out a fast and furious beat for the "modern" folks.

Lomé, Togo: In Togo, my daughter, Jessica, and I came home from the embassy each day at noon for some salad and baguette. Our server, Raoul, normally brought the food shortly after we arrived home. So far, so good. Jessica, however, liked to have cheese with her bread, but for some reason it was never on the table. The daily ritual was for me to "buzz" the kitchen (which was across the house from the family dining room), after which Raoul would reappear. Jessica would request the cheese, and Raoul would disappear. Four minutes into a task that would have taken Jessica no more than a minute, she would start wondering when the cheese would arrive; at minute six, her wonder would turn to irritation; at minute eight, she was on her way to the kitchen to get the cheese herself. This happened every day. Raoul was not being inconsiderate or lazy; he just didn't know he was supposed to run a relay race with the cheese and would get involved in a few other things along the way, such as a conversation with the cook.

This little vignette illustrates another aspect of traditional time: It not only moves at a different pace, but it can flow in more than one direction. That is to say, people in traditional cultures don't tend to dedicate a specific segment of time to only one task and proceed to deal with that task in a step-by-step, linear way. Many things can be going on at the same time, some personal, some work-related. The more traditional the context, the less likely it is that the local people will even make a distinction between personal and work-related tasks. They are just all things that are happening or to which one has to give one's attention. It's not at all uncommon for an African cabinet minister to have two cell phones and multiple "land lines" in his or her office, all ringing constantly and requiring at least brief conversations while some hapless diplomat sits patiently and waits for an opportunity to make the point for which he requested the meeting with the minister.

Baghdad, Iraq: *The only time I departed Iraq via the commercial side of the Baghdad International Airport was an American's nightmare, and not because of fear for my safety in wartime Iraq. The process for obtaining a ticket involved standing in a crowded room waiting to be served by one of two airline officials. The problem was that they were heavily engaged in conversation with one another, while taking apparently personal calls on their cell phones, sending their office boy off to fetch cigarettes and coffee, and having their attention distracted by the most assertive of the would-be travelers. Both officials were working haphazardly (to the American eye) on several tickets at a time. The Americans in the room were getting quite agitated – which didn't help much – concerned that their flight would depart before they could get their tickets and board. Then the two officials announced that they were taking a two-hour lunch break. Pandemonium erupted. In response to the travelers' fears that we would miss our flight, the airline officials dryly advised us that that was impossible; they were the flight crew. The plane would take off when all necessary functions, including issuing tickets, were complete, which, as it turned out, was several hours after the scheduled departure time.*

These points about time may seem pretty obvious, especially to those who have worked and traveled extensively abroad. Obvious or not, different concepts of time are among the harder things to come to grips with when you're directing operations overseas. You're on a schedule; people back at headquarters expect you to get things done. You might be working under a contract that obligates you to produce certain things by certain times. If the people you're working with and relying upon don't share or understand your sense of urgency, you're going to need to figure out how to get them to do what you want them to do in ways that make sense in their cultural context. If there were a magic formula for doing this, which regrettably there is not, it would start with gaining as thorough an understanding as possible of the local culture's concept of time. In that process, don't assume that the challenges are all going to come from cultures with a very different concept of time. Sometimes they will come from people in countries who hold a more extreme view of your own culture's concept of time:

> **Munich, Germany:** *When I served at the U.S. Consulate in Munich, Germany, we had many high level visitors from the U.S. government, which I'm sure had nothing to do with Munich's immense charm or the Oktoberfest. These visits or the demands they created would often arise on short notice and require jumping through flaming hoops of fire to accommodate. Shortly after my arrival, such a visit occurred, forcing me to engage the services of one of my German employees on a Sunday to make certain arrangements. When I called the normally very helpful, hardworking employee, she informed me that it was Sunday and that, in Germany, it was inappropriate for me to interrupt her enjoyment of her weekend, despite the unfortunate and poorly timed requirements of the unexpected visit. After a few tense moments, she agreed to do what I had requested of her, but I think both of us put down the receivers of our respective phones somewhat taken aback.*

Orientation to Society

When you think about your life or your career, where you are now, and where you'd like to be, who is the primary motivating force -- yourself, your extended family, your team at work, society? Do you tend to think in terms of personal successes, failures, achievements, objectives, etc., or your status

60

and contributions relative to some group? There are no right and wrong answers to these questions, either professionally or morally. What they represent are two different orientations toward the world and society and the types of cultures to which they apply: individualist and collectivist cultures.

In individualist cultures, not surprisingly, the individual is viewed as the primary driver of his or her own destiny. The socio-economic status of one's immediate family certainly has an effect on the extent to which opportunities might or might not be available to the individual. That status, however, is no guarantee of individual success or wellbeing, and conversely, the individual can overcome obstacles created by an unfavorable socio-economic status. Of course, the individual is not divorced from society; he or she will have to work and cooperate with many other individuals to accomplish goals on behalf of his or her organization, community, or country, but the individual's endeavors in this regard will be a matter of personal choice. The ethos of individualist cultures is that the individual is in command of his or her own destiny and should be all that he or she can be as an individual. There is a sense that individuals striving and achieving on a personal level elevate and bring prosperity to the community, society, and country. People strive to keep up with the high achieving Jones.

In collectivist cultures, the individual looks at his or her place in the world in terms of the extended family and society, or some sub-group thereof, such as the organization for which he or she works. The extended family is the protective bubble that defines who an individual is in the broader society. To a considerable degree, society dictates who the individual is and what it will be possible for him or her to do on behalf of the extended family and for the good of the society. The needs of the family and society trump individual needs or desires. In the collectivist culture, the success of the community will determine the success of its members, and striving to achieve individual success might not be encouraged, and might even be strongly discouraged.

 Rural Zaire: A *colleague of mine was a Peace Corps volunteer in Zaire (now the Democratic Republic of the Congo) in the 1970s. He worked on an animal husbandry project and helped members of his community establish*

61

> *small chicken farms, some of which were thriving by the time he completed his Peace Corps service and left Zaire. Many years later, he returned to Zaire and went back the community in which he lived. All of the chicken operations had long since collapsed, but for the skeletons of some cages and infrastructure. When he asked those who had built up successful businesses what had happened in the intervening years – expecting to hear something about some avian disease or drought – he was told that other members of the community had destroyed the farms out of jealously. In essence, instead of keeping up with the Jones, or the Kumalos, the village pulled them back.*

This story simply highlights the primacy of the community in collectivist cultures; it is not meant to damn them. In fact, among the many positive features of collectivist cultures is the great reverence with which people take care of their aging family members. What's more, generally no one is going to go hungry in a collectivist culture unless the community itself is starving.

While it's true that most traditional countries tend to be collectivist, it's not true that all modern countries have individualist cultures. Japan is a modern country with a culture that has strong collectivist elements, yet individualism is creeping into some elements of the culture. Likewise, South Korea has rapidly become a modern and economically vibrant country, but the collectivist culture remains strong.

So why is it important for the international manager to understand this particular cultural factor? Well, if you're in a country where the group is supreme and individual achievement may be suspect, it's going to affect (and explain) how your staff behaves. Why doesn't anybody seem to want to take initiative? Why did Mr. Akito seem so uncomfortable when I complimented him on his solution to his project team's problem? What should our organization's award and recognition system look like to take into account the local culture's group orientation? What kind of training program is appropriate? One that sends individuals off for training at headquarters or one that brings someone from headquarters to train a project team or work group?

Relationship to Authority

Do you call your boss by her first name? Do you expect her and other senior officials in your organization to consult you and solicit your input before making decisions that concern your section? Would you be comfortable challenging higher ups in your organization if you thought they were headed down the wrong path? Do you view government employees, at whatever level, as public servants from whom you expect service and are willing to demand it if you aren't getting it? If you're an American, chances are high that the answers to most of these questions are "yes," or at least a qualified "yes." If you're a Pakistani, that might not be the case.

One principal way that people from culture to culture differ is in their relationship to authority. This, it turns out, is an evolving factor that also differs within a culture across generations. In many modern countries (back to that imperfect term), people are increasingly likely to view formal authority as simply an organizing principle rather than something that implies social distance and limits one's ability to express one's views on operations. In fact, for the past few decades good management in these countries has been defined by inclusiveness, bringing people into the decision making process, to the point where now the question is sometimes how to reach critical decisions effectively without becoming bogged down with too much consultation. There have been more than a few episodes of "Committees Gone Wild," and some managers now struggle to assert what authority they might possess. In any case, people in many modern cultures have a pretty high comfort level with challenging authority and demanding that managers consider their views and concerns.

In more traditional societies, there is often far less comfort with challenging authority. The results of doing so in countries that have cultures that grant authority figures more exclusive rights to exercise their power can be bad: termination, social ostracism or worse. These countries generally lack the socio-economic luxuries that allow people in modern countries to be more relaxed about authority: economic prosperity, high levels of education, open political systems, unfettered media. In the absence of these advantages, authority plays a more defining role in society, and thus to challenging it poses a greater threat

63

not only to the person being challenged, but to those over whom that individual exercises authority and certainly, as noted, to the challenger.

We should emphasize that, like several other cultural factors, the relationship to authority and comfort or discomfort in challenging it or taking part in its exercise is a continuum, not an on/off switch. People from modern countries with long democratic traditions will tend to be the most relaxed about authority relationships and people from poor countries with very traditional cultures will tend to be more rigid in their observation of these relationships. Levels of economic and political development, homogeneity of culture, history, education and other factors will affect where countries will fall between those two poles. Again, it's worth noting that there are definitely differences within countries in this regard. Younger people often have higher expectations with regard to inclusion in decision making – certainly in the United States, in any case – and more educated individuals might share that expectation and feel less distance and more camaraderie where those with authority in their organizations are concerned.

In managing your overseas operation, you are going to want to know where people in your country of assignment, and certainly on your staff, fall on this continuum. Will your staff either expect to call you by your first name or be uncomfortable if you asked them to do so? If you prefer that people refer to you more formally, using your title, how will that go over? This is no minor point; the name "thing," is very culturally loaded. "Counter-cultural" formality can create unhelpful social distance (inhibiting team spirit and reducing cooperation) in some countries, and likewise too little formality can make your local staff very uncomfortable and send completely confusing signals about the type of relation you desire (and this is not meant in the sexual sense). Often, you'll be managing both host country and expatriate staff, further complicating the issue.

Lomé, Togo: Certain aspects of the American Foreign Service culture have a quaint, eighteenth century air about them. Ambassadors are the demigods of the system (God forbid they let this go to their heads), and Foreign Service Officers tend to show them more formal deference than is

64

common in contemporary American culture. The question always arises, What does the ambassador want to be called? At the embassy in Togo, I used a formulation that many of my colleagues at U.S. embassies elsewhere in Africa have adopted: I told the American staff they should feel free to call me by my first name when we were among embassy Americans. When people from Togo or other countries were present, however, they should call me Mr. Ambassador or Ambassador Engle (never, please, "Your Excellency," despite its widespread use in Togo and many other countries). Using my first name outside the American community would have diminished the dignity and stature of the American ambassador in the eyes of non-Americans present, and I didn't feel I had the right to do that

Beyond the appropriate use of names, you really want to know what those who work for you in your country of assignment expect. Do they expect you to issue directives, without consultation, or would they rather that you engage them? Everybody really wants to be consulted, whether it's part of their culture or not, right? Wrong. If you invite someone in a culture where decision making is not normally inclusive to help you reach a decision, you might flatter them and motivate them with your novel, titillating suggestion, or you might cause them to wonder if you are weak or lazy. They might be thinking, "You're the boss; you're supposed to be making the decisions. Don't fob your responsibility off on others!" You need to figure out what's going to work and what's going to have unexpected consequences and adapt your management style accordingly.

You also need to figure out how your host country staff members interact among themselves, based on their relationship to authority. How do your organization's host country supervisors and subordinates interact? Is it getting the job done? It's not unusual to find that the host country nationals who work for your foreign organization (from their point of view) have gotten used to working at least in part according to the rules of your culture. It might be a part of the job that they really value, perhaps because it empowers them in ways that their own culture does not. Thus, for instance, if you want to

65

solicit your staff members' advice or guidance, even in cultures where that is not common, you might be able to do so, but you really need to do your homework and figure out how to go about it without creating uncertainty and dysfunction.

Finally, in this regard, what does the host country's tendency with regard to authority tell you about interactions with people outside your organization? If you're not getting what you need from a particular government office, what are you going to do? One thing you'd better do is asked your host country staff members what's appropriate. Generally, they're going to have a much better sense as to what will work and what won't than you will. Can you send them in to fight your organization's battle? Well, if you're in a country in which people don't tend to challenge authority, maybe not, unless they have some culturally appropriate way to achieve the desired result. Once again, the message is to be aware that these factors exist and inform yourself as best you can about the local scene.

Inter-Communal Tensions

There are relatively few homogeneous countries in the world. Most countries are made up of multiple racial, ethnic, or tribal groups. In discussing religion as a cross-cultural factor, we mentioned the need to be informed about tensions that might exist between people of different faiths and the effects such tensions might have on the workplace. The same is certainly true of racial, ethnic and tribal divisions: Are there groups between which tensions run very high? Does this affect how they work together or who might be accepted as a supervisor and who not? Is there any reason one group might be jealous of another due to perceived favoritism within your organization? Does one group or another appear to be overrepresented on your staff? Who is doing your hiring? If the person managing that process is a host country national, can you be sure that job applications are getting through irrespective of applicants' affiliation? How does inter-communal tension affect your organization's ability to accomplish tasks and objectives with contacts outside the organization?

In most cases, it will be to the advantage of your organization to avoid any hint or suggestion that it is taking sides in whatever inter-communal tensions might exist. That means being very careful about what you and others in the organization say, print or otherwise make available in the public realm. It could mean avoiding contact with leaders of the groups involved in the conflict, or if this is not feasible for some reason, perhaps going in the opposite direction by ensuring that you openly meet with all sides. Beware of attempts by parties to a conflict to create the impression that your organization backs them over other groups. How could this happen?

> ***Lilongwe, Malawi***: *In the early 1990s, in the southern African country of Malawi, cracks started to appear in the grip of the country's all powerful strongman, His Excellency the President for Life the Ngawzi (conqueror) Dr. H. Kamuzu Banda, who had dominated the country for almost 30 years. "Interest groups" emerged, to some extent on a regional and tribal basis, to represent people who did not support the country's single political party. One group, AFORD, created the impression that it was favored by the U.S. Embassy by, among other things, naming as its Vice Chairman one of the embassy's senior host country employees. This put the ambassador in a very difficult position. Although he did not want to encourage the impression that the embassy was affiliated with AFORD, firing the employee for freely associating with an informal group lobbying for more representative government and better respect for human rights was problematic. When Malawi's interest groups were allowed to become formal political parties and compete in elections, however, the ambassador advised the employee that U.S. law prohibited employees from being officers in political parties and that he must choose (freely) whether to stay on with the embassy or continue as an officer of AFORD.*

Gender Issues

The role of men and women in society is deeply encoded in a country's culture. The role of women, however, has changed dramatically (in historical perspective) over the past century,

67

especially, but not exclusively, with the rapid development of modern cultures as a result of the Industrial Revolution. Although women now enjoy the same economic and political rights as men in many countries, there are still countries whose cultures and or laws impose stringent restrictions on what women are allowed to do. Can they work outside the home, or even be outside the home unaccompanied by a male relative? Are they allowed to attend school and receive an education equal to that of a male? Is any job for which they are qualified truly open to them? Will male members of society work for and take direction from them?

What does the culture of your country of assignment dictate in this regard? Do you have women on your host country staff? Are they in supervisory roles over host country male employees? Will male employees work without difficulty with a female expatriate supervisor? Are there any special considerations that you have to take into account concerning your female employees? Can they function effectively vis-à-vis host country contacts and entities upon which your organization has to rely to obtain services or implement its programs? You'll need to know.

Cultural Practicalities

Beyond the broad factors at play in shaping and defining cultures are the myriad results: the customs, habits, expectations and attitudes of the people. They define life's daily rituals. You'll never be able to learn them all, if they can even be learned, but understanding some of the principal ones will not only help you to avoid awkward moments and make you more effective in your work, but will enrich your experience in country. Fortunately, there is a wealth of country-specific information available in books, websites and other formats to help you navigate your country of assignment. You'd be well served to get your hands on some of this information before you board the airplane.

In addition to the information we have already provided in this chapter, here are a few very practical things you'd be well served to find out as you assume your management duties in your country of assignment:

- **Gifts:** What is the protocol for giving and receiving gifts? When are you expected to give a gift? What is it appropriate to give? Do any gifts carry a certain, perhaps unintended message (such as red roses, which signify romantic love in some countries)? If you are the recipient of a gift, does the giver expect you to open it publicly, on the spot, or put it aside and open it in privacy?

- **Hospitality:** When are you expected to extend hospitality and under what circumstances? Is it appropriate to invite someone to your home or to a restaurant? What is the expectation with regard to reciprocating hospitality? Do guests who RSVP actually show up? Do guests who don't RSVP show up? Do invited guests sometimes bring uninvited ones with them? Is there a culturally acceptable time to arrive at an event: early (yes, this happens), at the stated time, a bit late, really late?

- **The Employer's Role:** Your organization obtains the services of local employees and compensates for those services, but beyond that, what is the role of the employer? Patron, who extends fiscal and moral support to deal with personal as well as professional problems? Simply the person or entity for whom one works and from whom one receives compensation, but who otherwise does not intrude into one's private affairs? Is the head of an operation perceived as the "employer" (thus obligated to fulfill the employer's responsibilities) even though he or she might not own the organization or dictate its policies?

- **Commitments:** What constitutes a commitment in a business relationship or otherwise? Can you take someone's word when they commit to doing something? Do people respect the terms of legal agreements?

- **Corruption and Ethics:** To what extent is there respect for the rule of law? Is corruption widespread in business or government? If so, what form does it take? Is truth considered absolute or subjective (and thus malleable to the convenience of the moment)? What is the public's attitude toward corruption? Is it contemptible, tolerated or accepted? What does the culture value – wisdom, integrity, loyalty, competence, compassion? The answer to this question often takes much observation to ascertain, but it's worth starting to figure out from Day One.

Obviously, there are many more practical applications of the culture about which you will have to educate yourself to successfully lead and manage your overseas operation. In some cases, you'll simply pick up the information as a result of interacting with people in your country of assignment. In others, you'll have to dig, probing your local contacts, talking to other expatriates, and paying close attention to how people behave. As you complete your assignment and prepare to leave, returning to your own country or taking another foreign assignment, you will realize that there are still many things you have not figured out about what makes the local people tick. You have not fully broken the code, but with some effort, you will have cracked enough of it to look back on your assignment not only with professional pride for what you've managed to accomplish, but also with personal pride in the friendships you have made and the extent to which your inter-cultural experience has opened your mind and made you a better, more worldly person.

10:15 a.m.   *Meeting with Ambassador Engle*
The Care and Feeding of Expatriates

*I hate to call you at home, but we're going to spend the weekend
at the lake, and I forgot to request a cooler from the warehouse.*

*---Expatriate employee calling
one of the authors early one Saturday
morning in Ethiopia*

The typical manager of a domestic organization has
broad responsibilities that include ensuring that the
organization's employees have what they need to do their jobs: a
place to work, whatever equipment and furnishings they might
need, appropriate policies and procedures to ensure their safety
and security at work, a system for addressing human resources
issues, and adequate funding for all of the above. Other than
health insurance and a retirement plan, the organization's
obligations to its employees, and the manager's duties in this
regard, generally stop pretty close to the office door. With few
exceptions, domestic organizations do not concern themselves
with the education of an employee's children, where the
employee lives or whether his or her residence is secure, how the
employee gets to work and whether his or her car is properly
insured, where the employee and his or her family receive
medical care, and the conditions under which the employee may
buy and sell personal property. Employees in domestic
organizations would likely feel a management officer was
intruding into their personal lives if he or she were involved in
such matters.

71

This is not the case for the international manager. The "care and feeding" of the expatriate employees the organization transfers to its field offices overseas constitutes one of the biggest differences between the lives of domestic and international managers. Organizations operating overseas, and therefore their managers, very often assume some responsibility for their expatriate employees' housing, education of their children, local health care, round-the-clock safety and security, trips home for vacation ("R&R" or rest and recuperation travel), and even recreation in more remote, less developed locations. International managers get involved in clearing their expatriate employees' household effects through customs, facilitating driver's licenses and auto insurance, and ensuring that their residency status vis-à-vis the host government is in order. If there's an incident at an expatriate employee's house or the employee is involved in a traffic accident, someone at the overseas operation, often the management officer, must ensure the safety of the employee and/or his or her family members and square matters with local authorities and other parties.

> **Lilongwe, Malawi:** *Late one night, we awoke to a ruckus in the backyard, as our embassy-provided security guard yelled out and appeared to chase someone off of our property. Indeed, a burglar had broken in, stealing our stereo, my daughter's boom box (from the room in which she was sleeping), and my wife's tennis shoes (from the room in which we were sleeping). Lilongwe had long been a safe place, and the embassy had not taken extreme security measures, such as installing window grates and creating "safe havens," at the residences of its expatriate employees. Things were changing, however, and this incident was a wake-up call. Within days, the management section of the embassy embarked on a crash program to "harden" our residence and those of its other expatriate employees. Once the work was done, nobody was going to break into the bedroom wing of our house without a whole lot of effort, and that helped us to sleep more easily.*

Why do expatriate staff members often receive all of these additional benefits and attention? Well, partly as an inducement to take and complete overseas assignments; I'll talk more about that in a minute. The likelihood that an organization will take care of its expatriate staff beyond the gates of the office compound tends to increase the more challenging and different the host country is from the organization's home country. Then there is the expatriate employee's unique status: The organization has brought this person and his or her family into the host country, and from the host government's perspective the organization is "on the hook" to a significant extent for their presence, their activities, and the consequences of both.

Given the impact expatriate staff members can have on an overseas operation – and the international manager's time – I'd like to use this meeting to talk about why organizations hire expatriates to staff certain positions overseas, why individuals take these positions, or not, and what you, as an international manager, have to do to make all of this work. As is the case throughout your day of consultations with us, I'm going to speak in very broad terms, which I hope will help you to identify the specific information and guidance you want to obtain from your organization's headquarters about the management of expatriate staff before departing for your assignment.

Why Fill a Position with an Expatriate?

To explore this question, it might be useful to start by asking, "Why *not* fill a position with an expatriate?" Arriving at the right answer involves some cost-benefit analysis, in either case, and where expatriate assignments are concerned, the operative word is indeed "cost." Most of the time, it is extremely expensive to send or bring someone in from outside the host country to fill a position. As I noted, the organization typically pays for the expatriate employee's housing, education for his or her children, R&R travel, and whatever other inducements it might take to get the person to accept the assignment. In addition, the organization pays to get the employee, his or family, and some portion of their personal effects to the country of assignment, and back again at the end of the assignment. I've seen organizations use figures from $100,000 to $300,000 for the *added* cost (i.e., beyond salary and standard benefits) of filling a position with an expatriate employee. There are other reasons *not* to fill a position with an expatriate employee – violence against foreigners, the need for greater continuity, the need to blend in to the local culture, and even a host country's objections to expatriate staff (often in the belief that they take jobs away from local people) – but high cost is definitely at the top of the list; organizations don't make this decision lightly.

So if it's so expensive, why fill a position with an expatriate? There are, in fact, several good reasons:

- The expatriate might possess knowledge and expertise that is not available locally.
- The organization might want someone who possesses a thorough understanding of and commitment to advancing its goals and objectives by virtue of career service at headquarters and other locations.
- The organization might have a need to protect proprietary or classified information.
- The position might entail representing the organization's home country in ways that only a citizen of that country can do; diplomatic positions would fit this description.
- The organization might desire greater accountability for resources and actions that it believes it can best demand from expatriate or international staff members.

74

Although the decision to fill a position with an (expensive) expatriate employee typically rests with headquarters, a well-run organization will seek advice from the head of the overseas operation where the position is to be filled. That individual, in the process of considering the reasons I just listed, must also consider management factors such as cost, security, and continuity. If the head of the international operation is not directly responsible for management, he or she will normally turn to the management officer for guidance on these points. Thus, as an international manager, you need to be familiar with the factors involved and prepared to weigh in when your organization is deciding whether or not to fill a position with an expatriate employee. Keep in mind, too, that such decisions are not permanent, and changing circumstances, such as the professional development of the host country national staff, might allow the organization to replace expatriates with HCNs in certain positions. An effective international manager will be on the lookout for these cost-saving opportunities.

To Go or Not to Go?

If you're like Tibor and me, the excitement of overseas living is inducement enough to take an international assignment. I used to muse, only somewhat jokingly, that my employer actually *paid* me to work overseas, covered the cost of getting there for me and my family, and even provided us a place to live – all of this to be doing exactly what I wanted to be doing, where I wanted to be doing it. It hardly seemed fair to accept money to have so much fun, although this is not a sentiment I ever shared with our human resources division.

Those of us infected by foreign wanderlust are surprised to learn that, in fact, not everyone considering an overseas assignment jumps at the opportunity, but organizations that have operations abroad know this very well. Assuming an employee has a natural interest in serving overseas, or is at least not turned off by the prospect, there are still many reasons he or she might be reluctant to accept an international assignment:

- His or her spouse might have a career which is either not easily portable or which the spouse is not willing to put on hold during the time the couple is overseas. These days, the two-career issue is very close to the top of the list of reasons people turn down foreign assignments and careers that require them.

- There might not be adequate schooling at the proposed foreign location for the employee's children.
- Health care in the country of assignment might not be adequate to address certain special conditions that the employee or his or her accompanying family members might have.
- An employee might have elderly parents or other family members he or she doesn't feel comfortable being so far away from during the course of an overseas assignment.
- Some aspect(s) of the proposed foreign location might be of concern to the employee – cost of living, security, level of development – creating the impression that life there will not be sufficiently comfortable. If the employee plans to have his or her family members accompany him or her, this could be an even greater concern.
- The organization's culture might not value overseas assignments, such that taking one has a neutral or even negative effect on an employee's career. International work is not the central mission of all organizations that send people overseas.

Some of the reasons employees might have for turning down an international assignment are highly personal, and there's little the organization can do to address them. If an employee really doesn't feel that he or she can be very far away from an ill or elderly parent, for instance, there is not much the organization can do about that. Organizations do have ways of dealing with many of the employee's concerns, however. As an international manager, you need to know what your organization offers in this regard to ensure that the expatriate positions at your overseas operation are filled and that those filling them are productive and content.

Common Conditions of Overseas Service

The benefits and conditions of overseas service vary greatly by organization and location. The "index" organizations use to determine whether a particular benefit or condition of service is applicable to a given site is very often the headquarters location. Since expatriate employees are typically hired and assigned by headquarters, this is a logical approach. Say that, by way of example, an organization's headquarters is in New York. The organization has offered one of its employees – a member of its international staff -- an assignment at the organization's operation in Amman, Jordan. The organization will likely compare various aspects of life in New York and life in Amman to determine whether the employee qualifies for a variety of benefits – inducements, allowances, or services -- while serving in Amman.

Let's take a look at what some these common benefits are, keeping in mind, again, that they vary by organization and location:

Cost of living allowance (COLA): If the cost of living is significantly higher in the country of assignment than it is at headquarters or some other index location, many organizations provide their expatriate staff members a monetary allowance to offset, wholly or in part, the cost difference. This helps to address employees' concerns about the financial implications of taking an assignment in the more expensive location. Organizations often calculate COLAs by comparing the cost of a market basket of goods expatriate employees typically procure on the local market in their country of assignment with the cost of the same market basket at headquarters or some other index location. Some organizations use the U.S. Department of State's published COLAs for the locations where they have operations: [http://aoprals.state.gov/Web920/cola.asp]. Others do their own surveys and perform their own calculations. Either way, the international management officer must be intimately familiar with whatever process the organization uses and be able to explain to expatriate staff members the basis for the COLA they're receiving, or why they're not receiving one.

Hardship differentials: Some locations afford employees greater access than others to goods and services, high quality education and health care, and recreation and entertainment. The crime situation and the ability of local security forces also vary considerably from country to country. When an organization determines that a location poses significant hardship relative to life at headquarters, it sometimes offers employees assigned to that location additional pay – a hardship differential -- to serve there. Unlike the COLA, whose purpose is to offset an employee's loss of buying power in an expensive location, the hardship differential is not based on the cost of living at the foreign location, so the employee should realize a net gain financially. The purpose of the hardship differential is to induce employees to consider serving in tough locations that might otherwise hold little attraction. The operating assumption is that many expatriate employees would – all things being equal – opt for the Londons, Tokyos and Sidneys of the world rather than the Lilongwes, New Delhis and Asuncions. The truth is, service in hardship locations can not only be more rewarding, but can also afford employees more quality time for family activities and a more tightly knit, supportive community. The overseas operations management section – the one that you're going to head up – is usually responsible for putting together whatever report or information headquarters relies on to determine if a hardship differential is warranted.

Don't be surprised if your expatriate colleagues urge you to convince headquarters that your location warrants a hardship differential, or, if you already have one, a higher differential. They might cite examples from other countries in which they've served that were "much nicer" but had the same or a higher hardship differential. Such comparisons can be deceiving.

Addis Ababa, Ethiopia: *When I served as management officer at the U.S. Embassy in Addis Ababa, the post had the highest possible hardship differential in force at the time. Although Ethiopia was extremely poor, our embassy compound, at about 8000 feet in elevation, was a cool haven of flowers and tall eucalyptus trees (never mind the lack of oxygen). I happened to be completing our biannual*

78

differential report when the regional medical officer made his first visit to Addis from steamy Mogadishu, which had the same hardship differential. I had written the standard "this place is hell" report, and, nice weather and beautiful compound aside, that was not hard to do in Addis. The doctor, however, who had to sign the medical portion of report, could not put out of his mind our climatic advantage and his living conditions in Mogadishu. He asked me for more time to consider its contents. In the evening, he and his wife were supposed to join us for dinner, but I got a barely audible call from him about an hour before the event advising me that the two of them had eaten some local ice cream -- our material for visitors strongly advised against this -- and were deathly ill. The next day, barely back on his feet, he readily agreed to sign off on the differential report.

Danger pay: Although it would be a stretch to say that danger pay is a *common* feature of expatriate compensation, it is regrettably more common than it was even 10 or 15 years ago. Many organizations offer danger pay to serve in places where there is a distinct threat of being wounded or killed in a violent attack, kidnapped, or otherwise targeted by those who would do the expatriate severe harm. Similar to the hardship differential, danger pay is a financial inducement, in this case to serve in a place that virtually all of your friends and family members would tell you you'd be crazy even to consider. In fact, for whatever other reasons individuals might take expatriate positions in such places – patriotism, a desire to help, positive effects on promotion and assignment, etc. – this financial incentive has a positive effect on organizations' efforts to recruit people for positions in some very dangerous locations.

Housing: It is quite common for organizations to provide either residential quarters or cover all or some portion of the cost of housing when an employee serves overseas. Part of the justification for doing so is that an overseas assignment is often for a specific period of time and is therefore, by definition, temporary. As such, an employee might not have the option to buy a house and settle down as one might in a more open-ended

79

domestic assignment. Foreign real estate and rental markets can also be very different than what employees are accustomed to at home -- some absurdly expensive, and some very complicated by domestic standards. The organization doesn't want an employee contemplating an international assignment to be turned off by the prospect of subjecting oneself and one's family to the host country's housing market, at least without financial assistance. From the employee's perspective, free or nearly free housing is a big (often tax-free) financial benefit.

Not surprisingly, housing is near the top of the list of "hot button" issues for expatriate employees and their family members, who have very strong feelings about the location, configuration and quality of the residence they will occupy during their assignment abroad. In my experience, expatriate employees' expectations about their housing is directly related to the number of other expatriate employees assigned to the overseas operation: the greater the number of other expatriate residences one has to compare with the one to which he or she has been assigned or been able to rent based on his or her housing allowance, the higher the likelihood that the employee or his or her spouse will conclude that they have not been given their due. And guess who's going to bear the brunt of any unhappiness they might feel in this regard: the person responsible for management services at the overseas operation -- you.

So, if your operation doesn't already have clear and objective criteria for determining the amount of a housing allowance an employee receives or the quarters to which he or she is assigned, you need to establish them – as soon as possible. The employee's position or rank, family size and at-home entertainment responsibilities are typical criteria in this regard. If your operation has a pool of residences to which it assigns its expatriate employees, a housing committee composed of expatriate employees can take some of the heat off of you, as international manager. But beware: some of the most fractious committees I've ever served on were housing committees in which certain members had motives inconsistent with the responsible stewardship of the organization's housing resources or even the best interests of the employees to whom they are assigning quarters. In the end, your organization expects you, the international manager, to run an efficient and responsible housing program for its expatriate employee.

> **Lomé, Togo**: As too often happens among members of the expatriate staff, employees at the U.S. Embassy in Lomé used the summer transfer cycle to make bids on quarters that were becoming vacant as other employees completed their assignments. When I arrived at post as ambassador, a complicated game of "musical houses" was in progress, with all of the bruised egos and anger that one might expect. When various people started making their cases to me (bad form, in embassy circles), I asked my management officer to come and see me. She acknowledged that many of the moves had more to do with employees' personal whims and desires than sound management of housing resources, but then noted that the housing committee had approved the moves and that, since she had no vote on the committee, she was powerless to do anything about it. At that point, we shared a "mentoring moment," as I explained to her that, in my opinion, a management officer is never powerless and should never consider himself or herself the victim of a committee. If the committee is doing something that is disadvantageous to the organization, the management officer, who typically controls many, if not most, of the overseas operation's resources, has an obligation to refuse to carry out the offending action and/or raise the issue with higher authority.

Naturally, you want the expatriate employees and family members to be happy with their housing, but not at any cost. Clear housing criteria – and the gumption to insist that the operation abide by them – can help you to manage and temper expectations.

Dependent education: Many organizations also assist their employees in obtaining and paying for the education of their children, normally through high school, while the employee and his or her family are overseas. Organizations don't want employees ruling out assignments abroad because they don't

81

believe their children will receive a decent education in the process. In addition, if employees come from a country in which primary and secondary education are free, paying for their children's education while they are serving abroad will strike them as a financial disincentive to taking a foreign assignment.

Assistance with dependent education can take several forms: payment for education at the assignment location, payment for education at a boarding school, payment for home schooling programs, and payment of travel costs associated with dependent children's education. Let's look at some of the issues involved, keeping in mind that the management officer at an overseas operation is often right in the middle of them. Also keep in mind that dependent education is right up there with housing as one of the issues expatriate employees have very strong feelings about, and that's quite understandable, given that it concerns their children.

One of the first questions to address is whether or not there is adequate schooling available in the city or area where the overseas operation is located. In this context, "adequate" means roughly comparable in curriculum and quality to schooling that an employee's children would receive in communities near the organization's headquarters. Many cities around the world have international schools or other educational facilities that provide an adequate education by this definition, but that is not universally the case. As a general rule, the younger one's children, the greater the likelihood that adequate schooling will be available at the assignment location, assuming the overseas operation is located in a major city in the country of assignment. In places with relatively small international communities – and many developing countries still fit this description – adequate schooling at the secondary level (i.e., beyond eighth grade) can be a problem. For example, the U.S. Department of State's Office of Overseas Schools considers only four or five high schools in Sub-Saharan Africa reasonably comparable in curriculum and quality to high schools in the United States. By the way, the Office of Overseas Schools maintains a website, http://www.state.gov/m/a/os/index.htm, which provides information on expatriate schooling options around the world. This can be a useful resource for you and expatriates parents in your organization.

If there is an adequate school or schools in the area

where your overseas operation is located, you are going to want to ensure that your expatriate employees' children can gain admission. Often, these schools have a limited capacity and demand for enrollment is high. Some organizations – e.g., U.S. diplomatic and consular posts, multinational firms – provide grants and support to schools attended by a large number of their expatriate children to ensure continued access. When one large U.S. firm established operations in South Africa, it gave the International School of Johannesburg a large grant to construct an auditorium and several classrooms, thereby ensuring that its expatriate employees' 60 children could attend the school.

If the size of your overseas operation and the number of expatriate children for whom you hope to gain admission is small, you probably won't be able to offer significant financial support, but it is nevertheless important for you to cultivate a good relationship with officials at the school and be supportive to the extent that you are able. International schools in developing countries are often happy to receive tuition payments in hard (i.e., widely convertible) currency, so perhaps that's something you could offer. Sometimes these schools also run into obstacles vis-à-vis the host government and need the support of organizations with children at the school to make a case on their behalf with the right host government officials. You might also encourage your expatriate employees or their spouses to run for the school board, where they will be able to influence the school's academic and fiscal policies on behalf of your operation.

If there is *not* adequate schooling at certain grade levels at your overseas location, you need to know whether and how much your organization will pay for expatriate employees to send their children to boarding school. Some employees will not consider boarding school an option, so unless they are willing to home school, they will probably not accept an assignment in a location that won't accommodate their children's educational needs. Others are willing to consider boarding school if the conditions are right. Where are the boarding schools that headquarters uses to determine the amount of an "away-from-post" educational allowance, in the home country or at some regional location? Does the organization pay the cost of children's trips between the boarding school and your overseas operation? If so, how many trips per year does it authorize? You'll want to get the answers to these questions during your

83

consultations at headquarters or through your reading of your organization's regulations or employee handbook so that you can provide your expatriate employees well-informed guidance.

Beyond the concerns of expatriate parents wanting to ensure that their children are getting a good education while they serve overseas, there is one other important question you need to ask about your organization's dependent education benefits: Who pays for them? Are they paid for centrally, from headquarters? If so, you can breathe a sigh of relief. If the money to pay for them is in the budget for your overseas operation, however, you need to pay close attention, because educational benefits can be very expensive. Some international schools, because they recruit an international faculty, charge fees that rival college tuition. Likewise, the boarding school option, to include transportation costs, can have a significant impact on your budget. Since these benefits are a condition of expatriate employment, they are not discretionary expenses, but if you see that they are eating up more of your financial resources than you expected, you should request some relief from headquarters.

Health care: Domestic organizations often provide their employees' health insurance benefits, as do organizations with operations overseas. Beyond that, domestic organizations typically don't involve themselves in the employee's health care. The overseas operation, however, often doesn't have the luxury to "insure and forget about it" for a couple of reasons. First, the health insurance plan the organization offers its employees might not cover health care in all of the foreign locations where the organization has operations. Second, in some hardship locations, medical facilities providing care that your organization considers even marginally adequate are few to none. The organization has to have a "Plan B" to cover its expatriate employees and their family members in such situations.

As the manager of an overseas operation, you or someone on your staff needs to have a thorough knowledge of local medical resources. You also need to have plans addressing a wide range of medical contingencies and systems to implement those plans. If one of your expatriate employees or a family member falls ill or is injured, are there adequate medical facilities available to address the medical condition? The answer

84

is going to be different in Germany or Canada than it will be in Chad or Surinam. What if there are no facilities or medical professionals available in country to treat the condition?

> **Nicosia, Cyprus and Lilongwe, Malawi**: *My son broke his left and right arms almost two years apart to the day. The first time, we were in serving in Cyprus, and he had his arm set by a Cypriot orthopedic surgeon and spent the night in a clean, private hospital for observation. The second time, we were in Malawi, a poor country in southern Africa. Thankfully, our embassy nurse practitioner had a good knowledge of the local medical scene and was able to arrange for a Filipino orthopedic surgeon and a German anesthesiologist -- both in country under the auspices of development programs -- to set my son's arm. The large, public Kamuzu General Hospital where they performed the operation was far from clean and lacked nursing staff and medical supplies. Our nurse practitioner brought medical supplies from the embassy and was in attendance during the operation. Meanwhile, the embassy management staff was making airline reservations in the event that we had to evacuate my son to South Africa for treatment, which, fortunately, we did not. In both cases, the embassy covered those costs that were not covered by our health insurance plan. If evacuation to South Africa had been necessary, the embassy would have covered those costs for my son and one parent or a medical attendant, as well.*

If you're working for a large organization with many field offices and expatriate employees serving overseas, headquarters could well have a medical division to assist you in managing the medical program at your overseas operation. Some large organizations – the U.S. State Department, other large diplomatic services, the United Nations, the Peace Corps – assign medical professionals to their overseas operations, or sometimes hire them locally to run in-house clinics. These organizations often "self insure," budgeting for and covering the cost of medical care and evacuations from normal operating funds. Many organizations cannot afford or justify such a comprehensive

85

medical program, and if you're working for one of these organizations, you're going to have to be more resourceful in addressing health care needs of the expatriate employees and family members at your overseas operation. There are commercial insurance providers offering coverage for medical emergencies and evacuations from locations around the world and many organizations buy this coverage for their expatriate employees.

The old adage "an ounce of prevention is worth a pound of cure," holds special meaning in this context. Your organization's headquarters needs to ensure that it does not assign an employee to one of its overseas operations if that location is not equipped to handle a specific medical condition that afflicts the employee or one of his or her family members. That might require a round of medical examinations, but prudence dictates a thorough and cautious medical clearance process in advance of an assignment to a location that does not have medical facilities of high quality. If headquarters is sending employees and family members to your overseas operation without carefully considering potential medical issues (including psychiatric ones), I have two simple words of advice: Raise hell.

At the risk of being repetitive, health care is another condition of service about which expatriate employees and their families have strong concerns, for rather obvious reasons. You could legitimately ask, at this point in our discussion of expatriate employees, if there are any benefits or services they don't feel strongly about; I'd be hard pressed to cite one. But I think that makes the point: Employees serving overseas tend to be far more reliant on their employers for support than is the case when they are serving in their own country. You, the international manager, are providing that additional support, and as I said before, the "care and feeding" of expatriate employees and their families is one of the most unique aspects of international management.

A Few Other Things to Think About

Preparing for an expatriate employee's arrival: In an earlier meeting, Tibor gave you some excellent advice about preparing yourself and your family for your overseas assignment.

86

I now want you to consider that advice in your role as international manager. What can you do in that role to make the arrival of other expatriate employees and their families a positive experience?

Once your organization has decided to fill or refill a position with an expatriate employee and someone has accepted the assignment, you need to swing into action. First impressions are critical; you want the incoming staff member and his or her family to feel welcome and excited about the assignment. One of the best ways to do this is to open a line of communication with the employee as soon as you can. Whether you do this yourself or have someone in your management section or the new employee's section do this is a local call. In any case, via this communication you can come to an agreement with the employee about his or her arrival date and provide him or her preliminary information about life and work at your site.

Some overseas operations assign each incoming employee a sponsor, who is often another expatriate employee with a similar age-family profile. The sponsor can open up a less official dialogue with the employee, addressing personal questions he or she or any family members might have. The sponsor can play an important role in making a new employee, and his or her family, feel welcome by meeting them at the airport on arrival, introducing them to other members of the community, and helping them settle in during their first few weeks in country. Managing sponsorship programs is often the responsibility of the international manager's human resources staff. As such, it is something you can exercise some control over, and in that regard I have two pieces of advice: First, if your organization is large enough, try to select sponsors who are *not* in the same section as the incoming employee. The employee is going to get to know colleagues in his or her section soon enough; assigning someone from outside the section is an easy way to broaden the new employee's social network right from the start. Second, make sure that sponsors know how important it is to carry out their sponsorship duties conscientiously so that the new employee and his or her family have a positive first impression of their new assignment. Providing a sponsor a written checklist of things to do is a very good idea.

Expatriate training: Once assigned, the new employee will begin discussing training requirements (and ideally some training opportunity for family members) with people at headquarters. This is a dialogue the overseas operation needs to join. Training can make or break an overseas assignment, and as a general rule, you want the employee and his or her family to arrive well prepared to live and work in the country of assignment. Language training, cultural training and functional training are all part of the equation. Training takes time, however, often many months, especially if language training is involved. If your overseas operation is shorthanded, which is often the case, and training will result in a long period during which no one is filling the position to which the employee has been assigned, you might have to request that headquarters either reduce the amount of training the employee receives or send someone out temporarily to fill the employee's position. You only want to request curtailment of an expatriate employee's pre-arrival training if it is absolutely necessary to do so, and then one would hope it would be possible to reduce or eliminate the least useful training the employee is scheduled to take.

> **Baghdad, Iraq**: Serving as management counselor at the U.S. Embassy in Baghdad, inside the heavily fortified and misnamed Green Zone (it wasn't green), I was constantly recruiting people for one-year assignments. At one point, an incoming employee wanted to delay his arrival by two weeks to take a Middle Eastern area studies course. Since the employees duties were entirely internal to the embassy – i.e., the person's function did not involve extensive contact with Iraqis – I had to ask headquarters to nix that training, because we could not afford the staffing gap. My snide remark at the time was that, given the employee's internal duties, he would be better off taking Texas and Oklahoma studies, since many of the contractors providing service to the embassy came from those two states via their Houston-based employer. Under normal circumstances, I would have encouraged the employee to take the area studies course, but circumstances in Baghdad were far from normal.

Conduct: As I mentioned previously, when your organization brings (or sends) an employee into a country of assignment, the host government often holds the organization responsible for the employee's activities. This can extend to the employee's family members. Add to this the complications that arise when expatriates run afoul of the law in countries where its application is sometimes random and unpredictable, and it's clear that organizations operating overseas have a vested interest in their expatriate employees' conduct on and off the job. Awkward situations can arise as employees and their family members realize that what would clearly be an employer's intrusion into their private lives at home in their own country is not considered so by the organization overseas.

Ideally, headquarters has discussed this dynamic with the employee before he or she has agreed to take the overseas assignment. In any case, I would recommend meeting with employees soon after their arrival to provide them country-specific guidelines and explain the overseas operation's policies and expectations where conduct is concerned. Both what constitutes right and wrong behavior and the extent to which the host government or public holds the employing organization accountable varies from country to country, as do, of course, the laws of host countries. Has the expatriate employee taken the time to inform him or herself, as well as family members, as to how the laws, customs and social mores in the country of assignment are different than those in his or her own country? The meeting is your opportunity to provide that information clearly and in a way that makes it clear that it's necessary for the organization to hold the employee and his or her family members accountable. In reality, this advice is as much for the protection of the employee as it is for the reputation of the organization.

> **Lomé, Togo**: *When I was serving as U.S. ambassador to Togo, two members of the American staff ran afoul of local culture by engaging in homosexual kissing in a local bar. Complaints from the Togolese in the tiny, "fishbowl" capital of Lomé were quick to make their way back to the embassy. My management officer and I discussed the situation, which could have gotten very messy as notions of U.S. civil rights and personal liberties collided with local*

mores and diplomatic relations. We decided that initially, the management officer would make a quiet approach to the individuals concerned, advising them of the complaints we were receiving. Fortunately, that did the trick, because those involved understood the unique blurring of public and private life when serving overseas – especially for an organization that's representing its country. None of us liked the implicit discrimination involved, but this was not the time or place to force that point.

The timing of expatriate assignments: In most organizations, headquarters is going to determine the length of expatriate assignments and the process by which expatriates are assigned. What you need to pay attention to overseas, however, is the *timing* of expatriate assignments, not only in the short term, as I described with regard to arrival dates and training schedules, but over the course of a few assignment cycles. In that expatriate employees often have assignments of only 2-4 years, the overseas operation that relies heavily on them, typically in senior and supervisory positions, has a built-in continuity problem. HCNs play a very important role in maintaining continuity, but they might not be represented in the management ranks of the operation. To maintain broad continuity of goals, objectives, policies and procedures, you need to ensure that expatriate assignments are staggered so that not everyone in a section or in a chain of command is transferring out of country in the same cycle. Of course, the shorter the expatriate's length of tour, the harder it is to stagger expatriate arrivals and departures. In any case, this is something you need to keep an eye on.

Nicosia, Cyprus: When I arrived in Nicosia as management officer of the U.S. Embassy in 1990, the ambassador and the deputy chief of mission, to whom I reported, were new, as were the logistics and security officers, who reported to me. That meant that the five officers most heavily involved in management of the embassy were new. We made it work, but I know we

90

ended up reinventing more wheels than might have been the case had some of us in that group already been at post for a year or two. When I applied to leave post a year early to take a position as deputy chief of mission in Malawi, I successfully built my case on the fact that my early departure would break up this moving mass of key management officials, which the ambassador and the State Department agreed would be advantageous.

Getting to "Yes": As the person responsible for management at your overseas operation, you have a responsibility to ensure that the organization's resources – human, material, and financial – are used properly and effectively in pursuit of the organization's goals and objectives. There's no doubt that the extra benefits and conditions of service expatriate employees often enjoy can be very expensive and often difficult to deliver. There's also no doubt that you are going to encounter expatriate employees or their family members who, for whatever reason, are ungrateful for what they receive and whose demands seem to be never ending. Not coincidentally, people at headquarters and host country national staff members – two groups who typically don't receive the benefits that expatriate employees enjoy – often consider expatriate employees "spoiled." Sometimes they're right, but avoid being infected by this mentality, which is occasionally borne of jealousy. Someone in your organization thinks it's important to have expatriate employees filling specific positions at your overseas operation, and it's your job to support them. No need to editorialize, even mentally, on their presence or existence.

There will, nevertheless, be times when you are going to have to deny an expatriate employee's valid request, perhaps because you lack the resources to grant it, your organization's rules prohibit you from doing so, or for operational reasons the request is not in the organization's best interests. At those times, rather than simply say "no," try to work with the employee to explore the nature of the request and determine whether there is some way you can satisfy the real need without putting your organization at a disadvantage. Whether you arrive at a good solution or not, the person making the request will appreciate interest in his or her situation and your desire to be helpful. I've

91

heard too many management officers referred to as "Dr. No."

Munich, Germany: *When I was serving as junior officer at the U.S. Consulate General in Munich, the management section received a nice windfall of unspent funds from the embassy with instructions to spend it by midnight on September 30, the end of the fiscal year. The consulate's 50 or so apartments lacked dishwashers – somewhat anachronistically, as it was the 1980s – so my boss, the management officer, and I decided to use the money to purchase and install them. The employees and their families were delighted, with the exception of two, single junior officers, who complained that they needed cabinet space more than dishwashers and would not be able to take time away from the office to be present at their apartments for the installation. My problem was that I didn't want to have two apartments out of 50 without a dishwasher – both officers were scheduled to leave over the next two years – and I was afraid that if I simply put those dishwashers in the warehouse for later installation, they might not be there when I needed them. I told the two disgruntled officers that I could arrange for someone from my general services staff to be present for the installation, so that they did not have to take time away from their work. That left the cabinet space problem. If they didn't intend to use the machines to wash their dishes, I asked, why couldn't they store their kitchen items in the dishwashers, whose racks were well suited to this purpose? One of the officers thought I was joking and started to get angry, until the other officer pointed out that I serious, and that my suggestion was an excellent solution to their problem (and mine).*

Respect for host country national employees (HCNs) and reducing tensions: HCNs are almost always on a different compensation plan than expatriate employees. Overseas operations typically provide them different, normally fewer, services than they provide expatriate employees, on the notion that it has hired them locally and there is less need, either

92

legally or for practical reasons, to compensate for any differences in living conditions between the host country and headquarters. In addition, it is often the case that the operation's expatriate employees are in the supervisory positions. Finally, the expatriates are an island of foreigners in the host country, which sometimes (somewhat sadly) causes them to stick together for psychological and cultural comfort.

Do you see a recipe for expatriate-HCN tension here? You should. Again, an ounce of prevention is worth a pound of cure. It's highly likely that you won't be in a position to change the structural circumstances that cause some of this tension. What you can do, however, is to help each group understand the challenging circumstance under which the other works, and the basis behind the different compensation and services they receive. In this case, I think it is particularly important to ensure that the expatriate employees and their families appreciate the unique and very valuable contribution the HCNs make to the overseas operation. In most cases, the operation cannot function without them, and in some cases, they work for foreign organizations at great risk to themselves and their families. They might not always perform a task in the same way an expatriate employee would, but they fully deserve the respect of their expatriate colleagues and should reciprocate the same. This is the organizational culture you want to cultivate.

Islamabad, Pakistan: During my first assignment in the Foreign Service, I supervised more than 50 Pakistani employees in the general services office (logistics) of the embassy's management section. All of these employees were older than I was, and they knew their jobs and the history of embassy policies and procedures much better than I did. My right-hand man (i.e., the person who would keep this young junior officer from embarrassing himself), was a thoughtful and effective Pakistani employee in his 60s. One day, he was telling me about the string of people who had filled my boss's position and the Pakistani employees' reaction to them. In the process, he said something that has guided me ever since: "We really liked Mr. X; he always addressed us as 'gentlemen.'"

Moving out: Extending a warm welcome to new expatriate employees and their families is very important; and to the extent that your overseas operation does so, you increase the chances that these employees will be productive members of the team and have a rewarding experience. You also increase those chances by demonstrating that the operation takes good care of those who serve it well, and one very effective way to do this is to be supportive as expatriate employees seek onward assignments at headquarters or one of the organization's other locations. Being supportive can mean pointing them in the direction of good information about the locations they're interested in, putting them in contact with people in those locations, and even more valuable, contacting key officials to lobby on their behalf. There is often a culture that understands and supports this process in organizations whose bread and butter is overseas operations. But as I mentioned earlier, overseas operations are not the core business of some organizations that assign people overseas. For these organizations, overseas service might be an oddity that senior officials and others don't particularly value or know how to utilize effectively. If your organization fits this description, it is doubly important to help expatriate employees at your overseas operation obtain meaningful onward assignments, to the extent that you can do so. You'll build a stronger team as a result.

11:00 a.m.   ***Meeting with Ambassador Nagy***
                          Local Employees and Local Practice

Working for Americans is so different – they actually
expect you to work!

---Newly hired employee
to one of the authors in Togo

In the last meeting Greg explained the "care and feeding" of expatriate employees and listed a number of reasons why companies find it necessary to staff their overseas operations with other than host country nationals (HCNs). In this segment I'll present the flip side of the staffing equation – the critical role local employees play in the operations of any internationally based enterprise, the unique challenges they present to your corporate culture, and the difficulties they face in working for you. In addition, just before our meeting ends, I'll say a few words about third country national (TCN) employees: those who are citizens of neither the host country nor the United States.

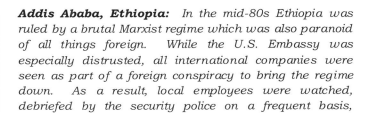

Addis Ababa, Ethiopia: *In the mid-80s Ethiopia was ruled by a brutal Marxist regime which was also paranoid of all things foreign. While the U.S. Embassy was especially distrusted, all international companies were seen as part of a foreign conspiracy to bring the regime down. As a result, local employees were watched, debriefed by the security police on a frequent basis,*

95

sometimes arrested, and occasionally beaten or tortured. Employees' family members were also subjected to these abuses. Our most senior local employee was nearly killed by a provincial governor while accompanying a congressional delegation to visit camps where U.S.-supplied grain was feeding famine victims. Another employee's daughter was arrested and raped by security police at the station. We did our absolute best to keep our employees out of danger by knowing up front that every word they heard us speak, or action they saw us take, they had to report to the authorities. So we watched what we said and did, and tried not to put them into any situation where they would be conflicted between loyalty to their country and loyalty to our organization. And when employees were arrested, we made sure their pay continued and their families had food, shelter, medical care, etc. When that government was finally overthrown, our employees bubbled over in their gratitude for all that we had done to help them.

Why Employ Host Country Nationals (HCNs)?

Put plainly, U.S. based companies could not operate internationally without HCNs. This is as true for Switzerland as it is for Burkina Faso. In most countries having HCNs is a legal must. Some countries mandate that a certain percentage of the total number of employees must be HCNs. In others, there is a requirement that certain work functions must be performed by HCNs (e.g., all drivers or clerical staff). In certain others – mostly developing nations -- the law may not require that current staffing include HCNs, but there are national goals backed by laws that direct gradual "localization."

However, even if local law does not require certain levels of locally hired staff, having HCNs makes operational sense. These are the people who speak the language, understand the culture, know how formal and informal systems operate, can get things done, know where to go in case of trouble, etc. I have seen over and over the tremendous problems foreign organizations have faced in simply trying to accomplish the most routine tasks when they did not have adequate HCN staff. During the Soviet era, for example, Soviet embassies rarely engaged local staff for even the most basic functions – including drivers and gardeners. My Soviet colleagues were forever complaining that their drivers could not make deliveries since they couldn't ask for directions, or get the vehicles properly serviced because they couldn't communicate with mechanics. China's earlier efforts with international contracts ran into similar problems. Chinese firms invariably underbid others by counting on importing large numbers of Chinese workers in all categories – from engineers to construction workers – to complete the job. The Chinese won many contracts, but a number of major projects ran into problems when there were culture clashes, some violent, with local residents because the Chinese workers either ignored or were ignorant of local sensitivities. In such cases, hiring HCNs could have easily prevented such problems.

Conakry, Guinea: My German colleague and I arrived around the same time to take over our embassies in Conakry, Guinea – known as one of the harshest cities in the world for quality of life because of its lack of basic infrastructure. Electricity was rarely generated, water almost never came out of the tap, potholes accumulated on potholes, and telephones were almost non-existent. Both he and I decided we had to have phones (and we're talking ancient landlines; there were no mobile phones at all!) to conduct our business, but we went about acquiring them in very different ways. He followed the formal method, writing a request and forwarding it to the telephone company through the prescribed government channels. I, on the other hand, passed the word among our long serving, and well-connected, local staff that I really needed a phone. Immediately one of our Guinean employees came forward to say that he had a relative who was an executive with the phone company, and he would take care of it. I had my phone within the week, while my German colleague was still waiting when his term ended two years later, despite numerous follow-up letters. In such cases, HCNs make all the difference.

The above example is typical of hundreds of similar cases where I've seen the direct benefits from an effective HCN staff. Most cases involved making life easier (or bearable) in a hostile environment, or enabling the organization to operate more effectively (or at all). A great many also involved preventing, or defusing cultural misunderstandings which could have led to varying degrees of embarrassment, unpleasantness, or even violence. And several were literally life-saving events: locating a local doctor after a car accident and being able to describe exactly the injuries and symptoms; passing safely through a road checkpoint manned by drunken soldiers, waving loaded semiautomatic rifles while looking for mercenaries who happened to be tall, bearded Caucasians (as am I); or translating correctly the warnings of a local goat herder that the roadside where I was planning to take a desperately needed "rest stop" still contained land mines.

Operating with HCNs – Not Easy for Anyone

Despite the advantages I cite above, the presence of local employees can cause significant complications. As I noted in the first example above, HCNs of American organizations operating abroad face formidable and unique challenges. They have to leave their language (even if the official language of the host country is "English"), culture, work habits, sometimes even their most fundamental beliefs at the company door. They may have to work together with ethnic groups which have been their historical rivals, or even blood enemies. Some of the rules and regulations governing their work and workplace behavior will seem illogical and incomprehensible within their own value systems. Some of the overarching principles of the organization's practices may be viscerally offensive (e.g., non-discrimination based on sex, or benefits for same-sex partners). And, as cited by the above example, if the host country government is of a form very different from ours or hostile to our country's government and fundamental beliefs, local employees will feel pressure from competing loyalties. The workplace will never totally reflect either the host nation's culture, or that of its U.S. headquarters. Instead, it will be a hybrid environment in which neither the local employees, nor the expatriate staff (U.S. and third country) will be totally at ease, and everyone will feel as if the operation could work so much more smoothly if only there were no (name the appropriate nationality or ethnic group) in the workforce. As a manager, one of your key challenges will be to make sure that your local employees fit as smoothly as possible into your organization's structure, are made to feel as equal and valuable components of your organization, are respected culturally, ethnically and linguistically, and are made aware that you recognize the inherent difficulties they face because of potential dual-loyalties.

99

***Lusaka, Zambia:** As I noted earlier, my first overseas posting was to Lusaka, Zambia – officially an "English" speaking nation. However, as I learned quickly, "English" is in no way a unitary language, and words have many different meanings. My first day in the office my very attractive Zambian secretary did her best to make me feel welcome and show me around the premises. After the tour, as she was leaving me in my office to deal with the stack of papers, she smiled and said "If you need me just give me a tinkle or knock me up." I know I turned crimson but did my best to keep a poker face. As quickly as I could I related her parting words to an American colleague, who just laughed and told me that my secretary was telling me in the local version of English that I could ring her extension if I needed her, or just call out for her to come into the office. While I encountered similar situations with my HCNs in my other "English" speaking postings, none provided the shock value as much as my first encounter with non-American English idioms!*

HCNs and Your Organizational Structure – You're Not in Kansas Any More

All organizations have formal and informal structures – whether related to position hierarchies, decision making, communications, or the chain of command. And all good managers understand that they must use both to effectively run their organization, especially since the informal structure can be much more important to smooth operations and effective communication than the formal. The international operation's informal structure is much more complicated than the U.S. version because of the presence of HCNs and the additional factors they present, be it language, culture, religion, or legal framework. Since you as the U.S. manager – especially if you are undertaking your first overseas posting – will be largely blind to some of these factors, it is critically important get a sense as quickly as possible of the informal structure and figure out how it works, who is really important, and how to use it to your

100

advantage. While very few managers are expert in the history, politics, sociology, linguistics, ethnic studies, or cultural studies of their country of assignment, you need to acquire at least a rudimentary background to avoid making serious misjudgments. Following are some criteria to consider when learning about your informal organizational structure;

- In many traditional societies age matters. In such circumstances, younger HCN's, even if in a formally higher status, will find it most difficult to give orders to, or discipline, older workers.

- Are your HCNs from a single ethnicity or multiple ethnic groups? If multiple, is there a pecking order of ethnic groups within the country – either historical or based on current politics? Is there a history of violence or subjugation among the groups? You can bet that whatever sense of hierarchy exists within the country will also be reflected within your organization, irrespective of any "equality" campaigns.

- Even if your employees all share a single ethnicity, consider religious affiliation. If they are all of the same religious faith, look at geographic origin. Despite official government policies or pronouncements, I have yet to find any nation where there is not at least one major self-identified factor within the population to denote "superiority" and "inferiority." This could be as esoteric as the village of someone's family origin. In Guinea, for example, one of my brightest and most energetic employees received no respect from the rest of the staff. I couldn't figure it out, because he was a Muslim and from one of the leading ethnic groups. Finally a local employee told me that his family originated from a village whose inhabitants had been slaves in the 18th century – and the stigma continued to the present day, despite a college education!

- The same criteria often apply to sexual discrimination. In some societies women continue to be treated – either *de jure* or *de facto* or both -- as

101

second class citizens (or worse), and those attitudes will not magically change at your organization's door. Discrimination and open hostility can be even more dramatic on issues of sexual orientation. While your official in-house policies may forbid discrimination, unless the laws of your host country make it impossible for you to promote equal treatment, your organization's informal structure will very much reflect the national sentiment.

Lomé, Togo: The long-serving President of Togo was from a Northern ethnic group, while the embassy was located in the more urbane and educated South. When I arrived I quickly learned that all of our HCNs were Southerners – and since our local personnel officer was from the South, this was not going to change without effort. Despite huge resistance from the local staff, I mandated that new hires had to be from Togolese ethnic groups who were not represented on the staff (i.e., Northerners). The complaints I received included: "they are uneducated, lazy, thieves, untrustworthy," and the like. It took constant pushing on my part, but we finally hired some Northern drivers and a few clerical staff. Amazingly, word even got to the President of my efforts – and he was greatly pleased, as were the other Northern ministers. One immediate benefit was that whenever we traveled to the North, we could take a driver who spoke the local language and knew the local customs – and could negotiate for gasoline and food and other services at much better rates than we had paid before. There are huge advantages to having a local staff which represents all segments of the host country.

While implementing such an "affirmative action" program may be your eventual goal, your most immediate concern is making sense of your informal HCN structure. Use several sources of information when figuring out how it works, since chances are – especially when soliciting information from

102

HCNs – that you will be getting a very parochial or biased point of view, especially regarding the interlocutor's ethnic group, religion, geographic origin, etc. But once you know which HCNs are your most influential, and how your HCN staff is grouped, you can start using that information to improve your organization's performance, morale, and internal communications.

When you have a staff with sharp ethnic and/or religious divides, don't take sides. Be as neutral as possible; never make negative comments about one ethnic group to a member of another. They know you are an American, and would be delighted if you favored their own group, but will accept your neutrality. It will be disastrous if you become identified with one segment or another. Especially in developing nations, sudden power shifts can occur – and if you're known as being partial to group X, and group Y or Z takes over, your effectiveness will be greatly diminished. In all my postings my family and I were known to attend Christian services and to be friends with American missionaries. But I also treated my Islamic, Bahai, Hindu, etc. employees with the highest respect and never favored one religion over another. I also visited mosques and met often with Islamic Imams and Scholars, and started every speech with culturally appropriate greetings (e.g., "Salaam Alekum" in conservative Guinean villages). This was greatly appreciated by the Guinean government and public, so the fact that I practiced a "minority" religion never became an issue.

> **Conakry, Guinea:** *Guinea has four primary ethnic groups – each with historic animosities toward the others. While Islam is the predominant faith, there are significant minorities of Christians and animists among some ethnic groups. Our operation included several U.S. government agencies in different locations. That, combined with our local staff's considerable ethnic and religious diversity, made it a challenge to figure out which HCN was considered by the rest as the leader. Asking questions such as "who can best explain local customs" and "who is most knowledgeable about HCN issues" eventually led me to a long-time employee of Peace Corps, from a minor ethnic group which had immigrated to Guinea from a*

103

neighboring country the century before. I found it immensely useful to use him to communicate important issues to the staff, and in return, he had an "open door" to bring me matters which concerned our HCNs. He could also explain to me why measures I was considering presented problems in the Guinean context, and I could equally explain to him why certain procedures had to be a certain way. By getting him on my side, I had the assurance that I had HCN "buy in." In Guinea's traditional, hierarchical, and ethnically charged context, trying to do things the "American" way would have been a disaster.

HCN Compensation and Conditions of Work

In addition to the obvious differences of language and culture, it is likely that your expatriate staff and HCNs will have different pay plans, benefits, labor organizations, and conditions of work. In some countries you will have little flexibility regarding your HCNs since the local government will mandate pay scales, working hours, paid holidays, disciplinary procedures, etc. In others, however, you will have considerable flexibility. Developing countries often present a paradox in that government regulations may be strictly written, but haphazardly enforced or implemented. Let's look at some of the major issues:

Pay: In my experience, HCN concerns over compensation consistently top the list of issues that emerged during my initial meetings with the group or their representatives. There are usually two complaints: either that they are paid less than counterparts working for similar international companies; or, that they are paid much less than the expatriate employees who do similar work. It's critically important for your organization's morale to address both issues. One of the consultations I routinely undertook before going out on my next assignment was to check the HCN compensation files at headquarters to read about any ongoing problems and to see what had been done recently about compensation. A good system to adjudicate compensation is to perform a "comparator" survey on a recurring, scheduled basis with similar companies and similar work categories. Three years may be a good cycle, but it should depend on local circumstances – the inflationary environment, the labor market, rate of industrialization or introduction of technology, etc. For the number of "comparators," five is ideal, but three will also work. Unfortunately in some circumstances there may only be one other company like yours; or even none. You should be careful to also incorporate benefits others offer; if you can't match them, then figure out a way to monetize their value and adjust your pay scales. Of course, there are so many variables to consider with each locale that it's impossible to touch on all – but the important factor is that if you have a systematic and transparent way that you develop and update your salary tables, your employees will be much more content.

Pay differences between HCNs and expatriates can be quite sensitive. While there are locales where HCNs make significantly more than expatriates (e.g., Switzerland and some EU countries), the situation in most countries is that expatriates are better paid, and enjoy benefits – such as children's schooling, home travel, etc. – which HCNs never receive. This is one reason why some governments undertake "nationalization" campaigns to limit or forbid the hiring of expatriates in certain job categories. Obviously you'll be working with whatever legal constraints exist in your country of assignment, but do remember that this can be a very fractious issue. You need to remember that the expatriate and HCN compensation plans are based on totally different fundamentals so should not be used as comparators for each other. The HCN plan is tied to the local economy – not what is happening at your headquarters.

Health benefits and retirement: Most developed nation's health and retirement systems either match those of the U.S., or are even more generous. In contrast, many developing nations have dysfunctional health systems and non-existent, or very minimal, national retirement plans. Aside from pay, these issues tend to be of great concern to HCNs in much of the world. In countries where these systems are weak, I have always tried to find ways to help our HCNs cope – which improves morale, and makes them more loyal and productive. Here are a few examples:

- In a number of countries we contracted directly with local clinics, hospitals and even pharmacies and, in effect, managed our own private health insurance system for our employees. Caution: In countries where extended or polygamous families are the norm, be careful to specify up front which relatives are covered (including how many spouses) and how many visits.

- In some countries without a working social security type system, we paid employees lump-sum longevity on retirement or termination which served, in effect, to fund their retirement years. In some others – where the law allowed – we helped employees purchase an annuity from an off-shore company. In any case, my experience has taught me that it is extremely important for the employer to make sure that long years of loyal service are rewarded, whether or not the local government cares about its own people.

- HIV/AIDS: Some parts of the developing world are experiencing an HIV/AIDS crisis, with some countries in Sub-Saharan Africa suffering from rates as high as 36 percent. While anti-retroviral drugs have made a major impact in recent years, a huge majority of HIV positive people still have no access to these medicines. Companies in such areas have undertaken several strategies to safeguard their workers (and the training and other investment they have made in their workforce). These include arranging their own medication for affected employees, and even double-encumbering certain positions knowing that high sickness-related absenteeism will mean that a significant portion of the workforce may be out sick on any given day!

Training – especially outside of home country: HCNs consider training a major benefit, and if you can manage to do it outside the country – it's even a bigger bonus. Sometimes U.S. visa restrictions can be quite severe, which makes it even more beneficial to use a third country as a training destination.

Another benefit to using a non-U.S. training destination is to discourage your employees from overstaying their U.S. visas, which leads to loss of credibility with the local U.S. Embassy and greater difficulties for future visa requests.

Awards: As in the United States, awards can serve as a major motivator for the HCN staff. The more ceremonial the culture (e.g., East Asia) the more effort should go into an award ceremony. I always insisted on having a joint ceremony with expatriate staff and HCNs receiving their awards together, followed by a reception. This was always a great method for sending the signal that despite the differences in national origin, everyone was on the same team.

Employment taxes: Again, there is a huge difference between developed countries, with efficient and transparent tax systems, and developing countries where there can be a high degree of corruption, dysfunction, and capriciousness. I have always tried to help our local employees – not to evade legitimate taxes – but to not be victimized by corrupt or non-working tax systems. You obviously have to be careful to follow the law – but use whatever flexibility you can to keep your HCNs from being victimized. For example, in some countries we provided to the local government the names of our employees, but not their salaries – or just their base pay, but not the value of their benefits. (Note: diplomatic   offices   and   international organizations often have immunity from having to provide certain employee information to the host government, a privilege private businesses and non-governmental organizations do not have.)

Employee organizations: HCNs invariably want to be organized, and here again, you have to be careful to comply with local law. Some governments are eager for your employees to be organized, others are most eager that they not. I found it useful for our HCNs to have some type of association – since it was an excellent means of two-way communication, and a quick way to learn what really concerned our local staff. In Cameroon, I even helped our employees establish an association, working with them on the charter – to make sure all ethnic groups and women had equal access – and served as an "election monitor" for their

107

first leadership vote. That the organization quickly became quite adversarial didn't bother me – the time I had to spend dealing with a series of issues was more than compensated for by our improved communications and the huge morale boost it gave our HCNs.

Holidays: You will have to decide which holidays to celebrate: U.S., local, both, or a mix. Some countries mandate the holidays which have to be given to employees, while others don't.   In still others, it seems that every other day is a "legitimate" holiday.   And to squeeze you from the other direction, some companies limit the number of holidays which can be taken at their facilities. Unless you are completely constrained by local law, I found the best way to be Solomonaic is to do the following: first, decide the maximum number of days you can give off; next, identify the major holidays which are celebrated both in the U.S. and locally, and put those on the list; then task your local employee organization and your expatriates to prioritize the remainder, and simply pick them off each list until you've reached your maximum number. This way everyone has buy-in on the list.

Conduct and discipline: This is another area where U.S. culture can clash dramatically with local standards. My first quote at the start of the session from our newly hired political assistant in Togo – whom I'll call Kofi - is something I heard at post after post from local employees. Compared to most cultures, we are workaholics, and we expect results – regardless of impediments. One of Kofi's first shocks was that when I sent him on in-country travel, there was no "recuperation" time off the day after he returned; he was expected back in the office. Another major adjustment was that if I sent him out to do a task, I expected that it would be done. As he phrased it: "If my car breaks down, I'll have to catch a taxi; if that breaks down, I'll have to walk - but no matter what, I have to do it!!!" And Kofi's greatest challenge was that when I announced a deadline, or the start time for a meeting – that was a mandate, not a suggestion!
Even more serious than differences in work habits are differing views of ethics. In some cultures stealing from an employer is only wrong if the culprit is caught, and a certain amount is almost expected. Padding travel vouchers and other

108

expenses, nepotism and cronyism, taking home supplies, using office equipment for side businesses, bullying or sexual harassment of subordinates, unaccounted-for absenteeism, etc. are all considered "normal" in many countries. You, as the manager, have to be absolutely firm in setting standards and expectations, and enforcing them when they are breached. This is one area where no amount of "we just have a different culture" can be an acceptable excuse for breaching clear rules and regulations.

When crises hit. We'll be covering "crises" in greater detail at a later meeting. Regarding HCNs, when a crisis hits your location, you will need to make some quick decisions regarding your responsibilities to both your local and expatriate staff. In most circumstances, the local staff is actually safer than your expatriates – but there are major exceptions. For example, if the crisis involves inter-ethnic or inter-religious violence, some of your local staff may be victims, while others, the victimizers. To what extent are you willing to try and protect your threatened HCNs and their families? If it's a crisis which causes you to suspend or terminate operations, how long will you keep paying the local staff? These are contingencies you need to plan for ahead of time, and be ready to implement based on possibilities within your operating environment. For example, the U.S. Embassy in Sudan was closed for a number of years, but we continued paying much of the local staff. In return, they made sure the embassy premises and vehicles remained safe and secure and they maintained minimal upkeep, paid utilities, etc. When U.S. – Sudanese relations were restored, the embassy was ready for immediate occupancy.

A Final Checklist

In reviewing the above topics, I'd like to offer some suggestions that will help you manage your HCN staff and avoid some of the most common problems:

- Learn the culture. I know both Greg and I have said this before, but I can't stress enough the importance of this one item. If you really want to have a clue as

109

to what is really going on in almost every situation at your post, you have to be able to put it into some cultural context. After almost 25 years in Africa, I know how much I don't know. But I have learned enough to often shake my head when seeing how my fellow Americans interact with local employees or contacts, or how they miss the obvious significance of something important that just happened. I promise that every hour you spend on learning the culture will earn compound interest at a phenomenal rate!

- Meet your HCNs early, and then periodically. If you can meet them all in a group, that's great – if not, make sure you meet representatives of your entire staff – not just a few favored elites. Let them see you as soon as possible after you get to post. Tell them your expectations and idiosyncrasies, so it's not someone else who is "interpreting" you to them. Tell them early and often how valuable they are to your operations.

- Be as inclusive as possible in your company's events and activities. Be open about differences that are obvious to everyone. If the pay scale is skewed dramatically towards expatriates, for example, you only lose credibility by pretending otherwise – explain, don't deny.

- Learn the real HCN hierarchy and use it to your advantage.

- Be on the lookout for scams; I can assure you that there are some going on right under your nose. I always searched for scams as soon as I got to post and invariably found them. I immediately dismissed those responsible, which sent a message that I might look like a naïve American, but I do have a clue, and I will not tolerate inappropriate behavior.

A Word about Third-Country-Nationals

We've now covered employees your company sends from the U.S. (expatriates), and national employees of the host

110

country where you operate (HCNs). The other category of employees you may encounter at your overseas operation is that of "third country nationals" (TCNs): citizens of neither the U.S. nor your host country, who your company either hires locally, or from the U.S., or another country – including their home. TCNs may even be "stateless" – e.g., the many Palestinians who work in Middle East countries who have no real "home" to which they can return.

TCNs may be hired for any number of reasons. They may have expert, unique skills your company needs. Many developing nations have few HCNs with professional and technical skills – whether because few are trained, or those who are leave for better opportunities. In some regions local nationals have historically been restricted to lower skilled labor, while immigrant groups were the professionals and technocrats. For example, in East Africa most professionals and business people were South Asian immigrants. Or, as will be more and more the case, your company may have a global workforce with certain categories of your employees eligible to work anywhere, from anywhere.

While TCNs offer obvious benefits to your operation, they also introduce an additional set of complications. They will usually require the same type and levels of support as your U.S. expatriates, which Greg detailed in the previous meeting. At the same time, they introduce additional variables into the ethnic/cultural mix. They also may require a wage scale that is different from both your HCN and expatriate rates. For example, their wages may be based on Euro equivalencies against the dollar, or the local currency. Your HCNs will view TCNs differently from the American expatriates – either more positively or more negatively – given cultural, religious, and ethnic dynamics. If there is a crisis requiring evacuation, your TCNs will not be helped by the U.S. Embassy – you may need to try and coordinate help for them from a number of other embassies; not easy when every second counts!

In sum, your company can not operate in an international setting without HCN (and possibly TCN) employees. By managing them sensitively and sensibly, the combination of ethnicities, cultures, languages, and religions can provide a wonderfully rich and energizing human environment which truly defines the term "synergy." Conversely – and I have seen this –

the wrong management approach will produce an atmosphere where these same characteristics will be akin to sandpaper rubbing against sandpaper. The former is much more preferable for your operations!

12:00 p.m.   ***Working Lunch with Ambassador Nagy***
                                           Entertaining Overseas

> *After dessert I'll give you the signal - go to the electric box and flip the circuits so the guests will think we're having another power outage and they will all go home!*

> *---A U.S. ambassador in Africa to one of the authors, then serving as his deputy*

Some people actually take international assignments because they are attracted to the idea of countless cocktail parties, fancy dinners, official lunches, and similar "cookie pushing" events. While official entertaining (or "representational activities" as we say in the U.S. diplomatic service) can indeed be highly productive to the work, the allure quickly fades and "exotic" becomes "tedious" after the fourth "national day" reception of the week when the same people yet again spend fifteen minutes discussing every aspect of the rainy season's heat and humidity, while the Irish ambassador shows he can offer a toast, in Gaelic, lasting 45 minutes!

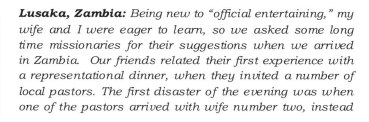

> ***Lusaka, Zambia:*** *Being new to "official entertaining," my wife and I were eager to learn, so we asked some long time missionaries for their suggestions when we arrived in Zambia. Our friends related their first experience with a representational dinner, when they invited a number of local pastors. The first disaster of the evening was when one of the pastors arrived with wife number two, instead*

113

of wife one, and another brought his five children in addition to his wife. After the hosts quickly added extra chairs, and rearranged place cards, the assembled went to the table. Knowing that Zambians enjoyed rice with various sauces, the wife had prepared what she thought would be a more than ample quantity by American standards. To her horror, when she passed the dish around, the first guest took the entire amount and put it on his plate, handing her back the empty serving bowl. She quickly had to go to the kitchen and cook up another batch while everyone waited. The lesson here – as with so many foreign "adventures" – know the culture!

Why Entertain?

Official entertaining is an essential part of working overseas – and the higher your position in the organization, the more of it you have to do. If I were to compare my overall effectiveness and accomplishments inside vs. outside the office, I'd guess it's about 80-20 in favor of outside. Of course, the major task of diplomacy is "representing" one's country – so managing an international operation would have quite a different percent breakdown. And much of that took place in venues which would qualify as official entertaining, or, as we say in the State Department: "official representational functions." These events encompass a great many types of activities: breakfasts, brunches, lunches, dinners, afternoon teas, stand up "dinnatoirs," cocktails, receptions, cultural events, picnics, sporting events, excursions, charitable events, and on and on. The common theme is that any enjoyment from the function is purely incidental – you are there because of your work: to accomplish a task, obtain information, pass on information, i.e., advance the interests of your organization. Here are some operational rules regarding "representation":

- Go with local practice: While some originality is welcome – especially in places where there is a heavy representational schedule (in Ethiopia there were at least two national day receptions each week) – don't stray too far from the norm. I moved from the Seychelles, where neckties are unknown, to Ethiopia, where men wore a tie (or national dress) on every occasion. Local practice also means going with expected times for arrival and departure, and, if local custom allows guests to bring unexpected family members, do a buffet dinner with open seating instead of a carefully crafted "sit down" dinner with formal settings and name places.

The Seychelles: *Our first dinner party invitation in the Seychelles said 8:00 PM – already rather late for our American habits. So based on a previous posting, my wife and I showed up around 8:30 figuring we'd be neither too late nor too early. To our surprise, we arrived just as the host himself was returning from the golf course prepared to shower, change clothes, and be ready to receive the other guests around 9:30. We thought we'd learned our lesson from this experience – until several tours later in Cameroon; we were invited for a wedding at 2:00 PM. We arrived around 3:00, just as the family was starting to decorate the church. The ceremony finally took place at 5:00!*

- When to be original: While we tended to follow local rules, we did make a few exceptions, and they turned out to be quite successful. On Thanksgiving – a uniquely North American holiday – we did our best to reproduce a traditional American style meal to which we invited key local contacts who had spent time in the U.S. This was always hugely appreciated and word got around the community to the point that many people were letting it be known that they wanted on the guest list for next year. Since usually the only thing the guests had in common was their time in the U.S., the conversation tended to be quite lively, with people sharing their (usually very positive) American experiences. Another event we repeated at most of our postings was a type of "game night." As guests arrived, we divided them into teams. In addition, we sometimes made them locate their dinner partner by making them half of a famous historical duo. After dinner, the teams engaged in lively competition – activities like tag teams running fifty feet and spinning around with a baseball bat – one end on the ground, the other on the players forehead - and then having to run back and tag the next player. OR carrying a ping pong ball on a spoon and passing it to the next player spoon to spoon. The evening concluded with each team having to come up with a skit – using a collection of props, which we usually took from our children's toy chest. This party was invariably the "hit" of the year – outshining any number of fancy dinners and champagne receptions. There was something joyful about seeing the Development Minister of the Seychelles trying to outrun the French ambassador while carrying a ping pong ball on a spoon in his mouth!

- What to serve: Again, going local is the usual rule, but there are occasions for originality. In Ethiopia, "national days" (like our July 4th) tended to be stuffy affairs with up to several thousand guests standing around in the back yard (outdoor spaces were huge) sipping drinks, eating the usual canapés, and boring

116

each other with polite chit chat. At some point, the ambassador hosting the event would read an overly long and tedious speech about the close ties between his/her country and Ethiopia, which no one would listen to, after which everyone would leave. My wife and I did the usual event the first time, then decided to change the rules. First, since the 4th of July fell during rainy season, we did our reception in February for "Presidents Day." Then, she planned an all-American menu: miniature hot dogs (all beef of course – given the large Muslim population), miniature hamburgers with locally made small buns and the like. We brought in an American musical duo to play traditional American music, and instead of the boring speech, I had our marines do an impressive flag ceremony; then, I exchanged a very brief toast with the highest ranking Ethiopian government official present. The party was a huge hit – even with the (uninvited) black and white Colobus monkey who came down occasionally from the overhanging branches to steal food and drink, and got quite drunk!

- We tried, whenever possible, to incorporate U.S. products into our menus, and the guests greatly appreciated it. I even hosted an American wine tasting in Guinea for the leading local supermarket owners, who were used to being sent the lowest quality European wines at premium prices. That was a huge hit and led to several of the supermarkets ordering California, and even Texas wines.

- Venues: I know it sounds like a broken record, but follow local practice – usually. I've been to posts, for example, where everyone entertained at restaurants over lunch. I did as well, most of the time. On occasion, however, I would invite someone to our house for a special occasion. When I was in Togo, I had a reciprocal schedule to regularly meet my Chinese colleague to exchange views and information. We took turns hosting at local restaurants. Knowing that my Chinese colleagues were not permitted to bring their families to post, I invited the senior staff of

117

their embassy to our home for a Saturday cook out where my wife and children were also present. They absolutely loved the informality and family ambiance, and in return our entire family was invited to their embassy for a twelve course dinner, which my kids absolutely loved (especially being expected to loudly slurp the soup).

- A word about appropriateness of venue or menu: I'm often astounded by someone's total lack of common sense – like when our USAID director hosted a reception at one of the most luxurious hotels anywhere, in one of the world's poorest countries, and served opulent fare to our development partners who were there to fight poverty and underdevelopment – evidence of a classic "let them eat cake!" attitude. The same thing goes for really stupid menu choices – like mystery meat in a country with highly strict religious dietary restrictions. But one of my favorite stories of poor menu choices comes from a close friend who was the Austrian protocol officer at U.S. Embassy Vienna for many years. Back in the bad old Soviet days, she was assisting a political appointee ambassador who wanted to provide an "American" flavor at a formal U.S.-Soviet "Friendship" Dinner. Despite my friend's advice, the ambassador insisted on serving the Soviet guests corn on the cob. Not only did the buttered cobs mess up the Soviets' white gloves, but they were insulted as well; in Russia cobs are only served to hogs! A good time was not had by all! Because of such really thoughtless acts, I learned that I had to spell out even such obvious "don'ts" in my representation policy (see below).

- Representation policies: In the unlikely event that your organization has an unlimited representation budget, this may not apply to you. But, at every one of my postings, I issued guidelines for my staff regarding representation, and included some of the following:

- Expense limits: Usually a per guest dollar limit by function, such as lunch or dinner at a restaurant, reception at a hotel, a meal at one's residence, etc.

118

- Overall limits by function (e.g., any function costing more than $500 needs prior authorization).

- Composition of guests: I required that at least fifty percent of the guests must be non-American, or fifty percent host country, etc. I did this because some of my staff were comfortable entertaining people like themselves – usually Caucasians from developed countries – but not as comfortable with host country nationals.

- Justification for event: (For government, or other highly bureaucratic organizations.) To be reimbursed for entertaining, my staff usually had to justify the expense by broad categories – e.g., national interests, promotion of U.S. products, cultivating a key contact, etc.

- Food for drivers: In many countries, most organization managers and local officials have chauffeurs, who end up waiting hours and hours while their passengers are wining and dining. I always made it a practice to make sure our kitchen staff delivered food to the waiting drivers, or I gave my driver money to buy his meal if we were out at a restaurant for a long evening.

Lagos, Nigeria: In Nigeria, not only do guests come habitually late, but they often show up with extras, including multiple wives. There is also a system followed by all – the more important a guest, the later his or her arrival. This works directly against another well-established practice – there is always a "high table" (literally placed on a long pedestal making it higher than all the other tables) for the VIPs. So as "important" persons arrive, they are placed at the high table, with additional chairs squeezed in as more important persons arrive. Eventually, there is no more room for especially late arrivals, who happen to be the most important, at which point someone or "someones" must be moved from the high table to a less haughty altitude. Of course, there

119

is always disagreement over who is of least importance – so the discussion can get very loud, and if there is shoving, some august personages end up falling off the pedestal. While such events can be quite entertaining at the start of one's career, they get old quickly. As I said at the beginning, entertaining is an essential part of the overseas posting, but anyone who takes up this type of work because of the "glamour" of it is making a huge mistake!

1:00 p.m.   *Meeting with Ambassador Nagy*
The Operating Environment

The quickest way to clear any shipment out of the Lagos port is to arrive with no document, just a truck and a wad of cash – and I'll have it out the gate within 30 minutes.

---Senior Nigerian employee to one of the authors on quickest way to get shipments out of customs

To those of us who have spent considerable time overseas, it's almost too easy to live and work in the U.S. Goods are available 24/7; public utilities work most of the time; emergency services respond quickly; driving licenses can be obtained without a bribe, as can shipments at the port or airport; and one can cash a check in most banks without enduring hours of shuffling between windows and waiting for signatures. Whether in developed countries, or the majority of the world which is still "developing," your overall operating environment will be nowhere near as convenient as it is the U.S. While certain aspects of living or working in your country of assignment may be superior to what you are used to, such as train travel in Europe or fresh produce markets in West Africa, there will still be idiosyncrasies in even the most developed environment, which will range from annoying to maddening (e.g., Swiss washing machines, which take three hours to wash three small items). Less developed countries offer even more dramatic

121

challenges to your operations and your staff's day to day quality of life. Greg and I are addressing some of the most important quality of life issues in other meetings, most especially "The Care and Feeding of Expatriates" and "Safety and Security - Job One." In this session I will only very briefly mention those factors, and then focus on issues which affect the ease of conducting your operations. In some cases, of course, the two aspects intersect, as in many overseas postings day to day life greatly impacts your staff's ability to work, and vice versa.

Conakry, Guinea: Of all my years in Africa I've never seen worse power problems than in Conakry. Instead of just going out for extended periods and then resuming, the electricity would drop for several minutes, then come back for several minutes, then go out again, and repeat this cycle throughout the day and night. The dry season was the worst, when we suffered the most erratic power. While all our houses and offices had backup generators, this kicking on and off – with its accompanying power spikes – burned out generator after generator. Freezers were also fried, along with computers, and air conditioning – essential in Conakry's humid and stifling heat - rarely worked. Understandably, our staff was becoming highly demoralized and requests for curtailing assignments multiplied. While I couldn't do anything about the city's supply of electricity, I could help our staff. We received authorization from Washington to install backup generators to the backup generators, and also added several large mobile units which we could transport to any residence or office complex. We also converted the generators, from kicking on instantly when power stopped, to a delayed start to reduce the constant starting/stopping/starting which did so much damage to electrical components. In addition, during the especially erratic times of the year, we simply stayed on generator power for most of the day. Once our employees had fairly reliable power, morale and productivity improved and for that reason, among others, curtailment requests stopped.

Quality of Life Issues

While the above example concerns a major "quality of life" issue – it also very much impacts your operations. After all, it's immaterial whether it is the curtailment of your expatriate employees, or the lack of consistent electricity -- your operations will be immobilized just the same. Other factors include:

- Infrastructure: the state and upkeep of roads, public transportation, air connections, utilities, and telecommunication services, including internet.

- Public health and health services: presence and prevalence of endemic diseases; rate of HIV/AIDS; condition of hospitals, clinics, and ambulance service; availability and quality of physicians, pharmacies and medicines.

- Safety, security and stability.

- Local culture's impact and limitations on your staff's life, such as lack of freedom of religion, restrictions on women, restrictions on sexual orientation, prohibition of alcohol, etc.

- Availability of recreational outlets and possibilities for practicing personal hobbies.

- Possibility of getting away for a change in scenery or environment, e.g., from the desert to refreshing mountains, and availability of cultural attractions such as museums, concerts.

- Availability and quality of goods and services.

Greg and I have spent many years at postings where the above factors played a major role in the community's well-being as well as how productive our operations would be. Be sure to give close attention when we discuss specifics at later meetings, because your success as an international manager will hinge on your ability to deal with these issues.

123

Factors Affecting Your Operations

Addis Ababa, Ethiopia. During my second assignment in Ethiopia (1999-2002), I was working with the most "democratic" government Ethiopia had had in its 2000 plus year history. It was, nevertheless, still far from ideal. Ethiopian officials kept assuring me that they were keenly interested in U.S. private sector investment – including having American companies set up operations there – but their signals were mixed, at best. One major irritant was that any time there was a dispute between an American entity (either person or organization) and an Ethiopian, the legal decision would invariably favor the local party – regardless of evidence. I finally reached my "diplomatic" patience limit when an American mission group, which had been operating in the country for many decades and doing wonderful development work, was in danger of losing its property. The Americans had purchased their property during imperial times in the early 20th century, but some fourth cousin thrice removed of the original owners showed up in a local government office in 2001 and claimed to be the rightful owner. It appeared that local officials would again capriciously rule in favor of the Ethiopian litigant and throw out the American group. In addition to writing the usual diplomatic note to the Ethiopian Ministry, I personally visited the local Ethiopian government officials in the area where the dispute was taking place; I assured them that if the mission group was ejected without due process, I would do my best to make sure that no American company ever invested in their region, and that U.S. government development projects would bypass their area. Amazingly (or not so), days later the local court found in favor of the American group.

As much as our embassies want to support the rights of U.S. citizens and companies abroad, our ambassadors cannot get involved in all such cases. Therefore it's essential that you, as an international manager, fully comprehend all the subtleties of your operating environment. Following is a checklist that will tell you just how challenging this will be:

- **Foreign government regulations and treatment**. This factor, more than any other, determines just how level your "playing field" is. While everyone has to drive on the same unpaved roads, endure power outages, avoid malarial mosquitoes, do without brie and pâté, if the local government discriminates based on nationality, your playing field is anything but level. Since so many factors that are critical to your operation depend on how the local government treats you, this is something about which you need complete information so that you are prepared. I've seen governments discriminate against Americans on issuing permits, tax treatment, granting of visas, clearance of goods from customs, zoning, land lease or purchase, and a number of other similar activities. Some governments also preclude Americans (sometimes specifically, sometimes generally for being "foreign") from certain segments of the economy, e.g., banking, telecommunications.

- **Local government's economic involvement:** If a government is heavily engaged in the economy, either directly or through its parastatal monopolies (export/import business, phone and internet services, utilities, beverage distributors, airlines, etc.), you can be certain that it will do its best – either through formal legal means or informal maneuvering – to keep you out of its areas of activity. Not only is it unlikely that you will be able to compete with a government parastatal, but you may have to buy certain products or services from them. And, invariably, they are inefficient and uncompetitive given their privileged status, with staffing based more on cronyism and nepotism than qualifications. In my experience, wherever governments participate in the local economy, international firms (and local ones) end up overpaying for inferior products and services, or find artificial shortages of essential products. In Nigeria, one of the world's largest oil producers, for example, gasoline is often unavailable.

- This also applies to the government's **currency policies**. I've been posted to countries where the government maintained a totally unrealistic 'official' rate of exchange, usually overvaluing the local currency by ridiculous amounts. A modest example: when I was in Zambia the *kwacha* was officially traded at 2 to the U.S. dollar, while the street value was 20 to 1. While individuals and small enterprises tend to ignore the official exchange rate and comfortably trade currency on the street, large companies – especially international ones – can be in the local government's crosshairs, and targeted for "currency violations." It's a difficult dilemma: follow official policy and be uncompetitive, or do what everyone else does and risk being fined, jailed, or closed down.

- Other currency regulations which will greatly impact your operations include: your ability to repatriate profits, and at what rate of exchange; the legality of paying expatriate staff (or even local staff) in foreign currency – something highly desired when the local currency is unconvertible or worthless; and your ability to pay certain local costs, such as leases, in foreign currency. If your organization is just starting its international expansion, and you have a set of regulations and operating policies based exclusively on U.S. operations, be prepared to revise them to be as flexible as possible, to give your managers on site the means for dealing with a set of issues you would never face in the U.S..

Lusaka, Zambia. As General Services Officer, I was responsible for finding housing for our embassy expatriate employees. The economic climate in Zambia in the late 70s and early 80s was a disaster – with a bankrupt, corrupt government incapable of providing services or maintaining law and order. Resident foreigners and the business class were in a panic to liquidate their assets and flee the country. In this environment I was able to routinely obtain large,

126

three/four bedroom houses on one acre of land, often with swimming pools or tennis courts, for about U.S. $35,000. Of course, the owners wanted the payment in dollars, deposited outside the country. Unfortunately our own regulations were quite restrictive – including having one account for purchasing property (which never had any funding) and another for leasing. And to pay outside Zambia in dollars was definitely a grey area of our regulations. I came up with what I thought was a creative approach – conduct the transactions as a lease, with payments credited towards the purchase of the property; while payments were in U.S. dollars, the leases stipulated that the recipients were fully responsible for paying all local taxes. The system worked great until our green eye shade folks at headquarters decided that we could not use lease payments to end up owning property, even though it was highly in our interest. Nor could we pay in US dollars, even though we were obtaining a huge savings over the official exchange rate. So we ended up just leasing, and paid considerably more for property we would never own.

- **Corruption**. Definitions vary, but in my view corruption is getting someone to do something they should be doing anyway; or to do something they should not be doing. Also, for a corrupt act to take place there has to be a corruptor as well as a corruptee. Corruption exists in every country to some degree, with the level and frequency dependent on whether or not it's officially and culturally repugnant, frowned on, overlooked, tolerated, accepted, or expected. Certain aspects, however, can make it very tricky:

Lagos, Nigeria. When I was posted to Nigeria in the mid-90s, it was the most corrupt nation on earth – a veritable kleptocracy. I was totally amazed and frustrated by the almost universal presence of corruption throughout every facet of Nigerian society. The best explanation came from Olusegun Obasanjo,

127

then under house arrest as an opposition leader – later to become Nigeria's head of state. I was the embassy's designated officer to occasionally visit Obasanjo, and once I shared with him my incredulity over Nigerians' level of corruption. He explained that when he had been a young lieutenant in the 60s and 70s, it would take about six months of his pay to buy a car; now (1994) a lieutenant would have to save his pay for ten years to make the same purchase. Given that soldiers had weapons, it didn't take a rocket scientist to figure out they would use them to shorten the purchase period! And according to Obasanjo, this same pay gap existed for all official salaries – whether for customs agents, immigration officials, police, license examiners, telephone workers – so they all used whatever power they had to supplement their meager pay.

This, of course, might explain why the drivers' license examiner asks for a small payment before giving the exam, or even provides the license without the exam, but it certainly cannot justify why heads of state of many countries, already multi-zillionaires, siphon off thousands of barrels of oil daily to grow their personal fortunes.

Being an American international manager puts you at a certain disadvantage since the *Foreign Corrupt Practices Act* forbids you from doing things your European, Latin American and Asian competitors do routinely. At the same time, there is a positive side that I found over and over: foreign officials are aware of the FCPA, and thus don't make the same demands on Americans that they would on others. In any case, do become familiar with the provisions of the FCPA to avoid problems for your organization and for yourself.

Yaounde, Cameroon. *In my various postings I found one group which consistently had a policy of never paying bribes: American-based missionary organizations, and individual missionaries would often have to endure*

128

endless procedures and bureaucratic hurdles which could have been instantly overcome with some cash quickly changing hands. Once I took a ride with one of these missionaries when he visited a number of his local churches in the rural areas beyond Cameroon's capital. Shortly after leaving the city, we came to the first of what I knew would be numerous roadblocks manned by uniformed personnel of various police agencies set up ostensibly to check our papers or make sure our vehicle was roadworthy, when in fact they were all looking to supplement their income. I asked my friend if I needed to produce my embassy ID and demand to be let through given my diplomatic status, and he said "Don't worry, I can handle this." To my surprise, at each roadblock he would simply hand out his religious pamphlets printed in local languages to the grim-faced uniformed and armed officers. They would immediately smile – regardless of their own religion – accept the pamphlets with a huge thanks ("Merci Pasteur!") and wave us through. The same week I had this uplifting experience with my friend, a potential U.S. investor considering a multi-million dollar investment in Cameroon left the country in disgust after having been shaken down at a similar roadblock for all the cash in his wallet – several hundred dollars. This illustrates one of Africa's tragedies – that a low-paid policeman can singlehandedly deliver a major blow to his country's development efforts through a case of petty corruption!

You will, I promise, have to deal with the corruption issue, and you will have to decide on the boundaries for your operation. My advice is make them firm, and draw them in a way that you'd have no regrets if your actions were printed on the front page of your home town newspaper. Your policies will, of course, have to be based to a certain extent on local practice. If it's customary to give the customs agents, telephone company employees, immigration officials, etc. a Christmas or end of year gift, then by all means do so. But even with such practices you

129

can exercise certain discernment. I was at a number of posts where international companies and organizations routinely handed out bottles of whiskey as their end of year gifts to a whole range of low-level and mid-level officials, technicians, etc., who provided essential services to their operations. My approach was – the bottle of whiskey would be quickly drunk and forgotten* – so I started giving out other gifts: watches, pen sets, caps and t-shirts, etc. with the embassy logo. My counterparts were often annoyed – one French colleague told me with disdain "I see the American Embassy logo in every office I visit," but it worked. In any case – good luck with however you decide to handle this highly sensitive and complex issue!

- **Know with whom you are dealing**: This factor appears over and over in our meetings today, but it is especially important in the overall operating environment. Irrespective of the inherent difficulties and complexities of your operating environment, there are key people – often in the informal, vice formal, hierarchy – who can make things happen, speed up the process, remove roadblocks. Get to know them! Conversely, be careful not to get into the situation of making deals with people who are not empowered to act, or are acting at a level above their scope of responsibilities. Most developing nations are also societies which use intermediaries to accomplish many important functions, including arranging marriages, dispute resolution, finding a job, etc. You will encounter individuals who will allege to be able to cut the red tape, make a contract happen, get the phones installed, etc. Be very careful. I have seen, over and over, U.S. organizations being victimized by signing leases and contracts with individuals who are not empowered to sign for the other party, and the agreements end up null and void. In one case this resulted in a multi-million dollar loss for the U.S. side. This is where your key local staff members, who know who is who in the local power structure, can be helpful, as can the U.S. Embassy commercial section, which can tell you about local practices. Of course, in developing world environments, even if you sign with the right government minister, there is no assurance that when the head of state reshuffles the cabinet, or a new government is installed through legal or extra-legal means, the new actors won't renounce your agreement.

- **Dispute resolution:** Given the operating complexities and inherent clashes of culture and business practices in the international environment, it's remarkable that there aren't more disputes involving American enterprises overseas. Based on some of the factors we discussed above, I strongly suggest that you carefully consider incorporating dispute resolution methods in all your important contracts and agreements which remove the dispute from the authority and influence of your host government, if this is possible. As I said above, while the local American Embassy does its best to make sure U.S. investors and organizations are protected as much as possible from the vagaries of the local "justice" system by demanding equal and fair treatment, this can never be fully assured. Therefore, contact an experienced and knowledgeable attorney who knows your country of operations before pursuing agreements.

Conakry, Guinea. The President invited me to sit with him at the formal ribbon cutting for a new hospital started by a U.S. investor. I've been to a number of such events during my time in Africa, and at some I was dubious about the chances of success. If the individual or group involved were neophytes, obviously naïve about how things worked, or were dealing with local agents whose motives were suspect, their great ideas eventually floundered. On this occasion I was more optimistic. The American developer, while new to Guinea, had obviously done his research into the business climate and identified local partners who knew how to get things done. He had also purchased the right equipment for staffing a hospital

131

(not the newest technology, but high quality products which could work in the harsh operating environment). What impressed me most, however, was the President taking me aside and telling me that he had personally followed the progress of the various permits and licenses to make sure they were approved swiftly and without anyone asking for bribes along the way. The President told me he was keen to attract U.S. investors, and wanted to send the message that they were welcome and would be fairly treated. So this venture turned out to be a success – but alas, even with the best of intentions, no president can be involved in monitoring the setting up and operation of every U.S. business venture, even in the smallest of countries.

Conclusion

I didn't want to mislead you by sugarcoating the seriousness of the challenges you'll face in your operating environment – but don't be discouraged. With flexibility, creativity, and knowledge you'll be able to overcome them. Greg and I have had to endure some of the most difficult operating environments in the world – and despite our share of frustrations, both of us have tremendously enjoyed our work been gratified by the successes. We would both do it all over again in an instant. Now it's your turn.

1:45 p.m.   *Meeting with Ambassador Engle*
                          Key Relationships at
                          Headquarters and in Country

It's not what you know, it's who you know.
                                          ---Anonymous

Washington, DC: *When I was Consul General in Johannesburg, South Africa, the building the Consulate General occupied was rapidly losing tenants, as were other buildings downtown. The companies that owned these buildings started to close them down as the cost of keeping them open exceeded the rent they produced. To avoid finding ourselves "out on the street," my staff and I located a building under construction just outside the downtown area and negotiated a build-to-lease option with the landlord, all with the blessing of the State Department in Washington. When it came time to commit to the lease, however, various players in the Department got cold feet. I went back to Washington and sat around a table for two days with about thirty officials involved in one aspect or another of the lease. Each official acknowledged that it made sense to move the Consulate and that the option we had developed seemed to be a good one; then, however, came the inevitable "but." By the end of the second day, we were no closer to an agreement. On the morning of the third day, I paid a call on the Under Secretary of State for Management, someone*

133

who knew me and my work and the official to whom everyone at our two-day meeting ultimately answered. I expressed my frustration at the process and the fact that, by letting an excellent opportunity slip away, we were at risk of ending up with no office space at all. Immediately after the meeting, I flew back to Johannesburg, where I learned that the Under Secretary had issued the order to "Make this project work." We moved into our new Consulate General fifteen months later.

Knowing and having access to the right people is important in both domestic and international management. As the foregoing vignette illustrates, the right person can cut through multiple layers of bureaucratic resistance, and if that person knows you and trusts you, his or her willingness to do so on your behalf will be greater.

I won't try to make the case that it's even more important for the international manager than for his or her domestic counterpart to have an effective network of contacts, because that's not true. I will venture to say, however, that in many cases the international manager's network is broader and more complex than the domestic manager's: broader because, as we discussed during our meeting on expatriate employees, the international manager's duties go well beyond the office door, and more complex because of the many cross cultural factors that come into play when developing these relationships overseas.

What I'd like to do during this session is discuss function and level as factors that determine who develops which relationships at the overseas operation. Then I will share my thoughts, almost in list form, on the range of relationships an international manage needs to cultivate to be effective.

Function and Level

The function and level of one's position in an organization – in this case, the overseas operation -- determine with whom one needs to develop the relationships that will be useful in performing one's duties. This should be a pretty straightforward concept, but in fact it's easy to interpret these factors either too broadly or too narrowly, and either can have negative consequences.

As an example, let's say that you're the HIV/AIDS program officer at the United Nations Development Program (UNDP) country office in Tanzania. You will presumably want to develop good working relationships with people at the Ministry of Health, as well as local s and private health care providers serving HIV/AIDS victims. The director of the UN's Electoral Support Program in Tanzania might, however, be surprised to bump into you coming out of a meeting with the head of Tanzania's National Election Commission. You might have a good reason for being there; perhaps you're working on a program that will take advantage of the upcoming voter registration and election process to distribute HIV/AIDS prevention literature. If that's the case, courtesy and effectiveness would dictate that you advise and consult with your Electoral Support Program colleague before meeting with Tanzanian officials who principally fall within his or her area of responsibility.

Conversely, if, as HIV/AIDs program officer, you define your role too narrowly or you're overly concerned about treading on other colleagues' turf to the point where you limit yourself to contacts to health officials and providers, you might miss some big opportunities. It might make good sense for you to be in regular contact with officials in the Ministries of Transportation and Defense, because in Africa, truck drivers and soldiers are often carriers and spreaders of HIV. The key here is to think carefully about your own function and those of others in your organization as you develop your professional network in country. Talking to your colleagues about who their contacts are and seeking their advice as to whom, in their realm, it might be useful for you to know is smart practice.

This applies, as well, to the level of your contacts and relationships. If you're a junior officer in UNDP/Tanzania's HIV/AIDS program office, your principal contact at the Ministry of Health is probably not the Minister, nor even, necessarily, the head of the Ministry's HIV/AIDS program. The director of your program – or in the case of the Minister, perhaps the head of UN operations in Tanzania -- has probably reserved those relationships for himself or herself. Inadvertently crossing

135

functional lines without proper consultations with your colleagues can cause irritation within your organization and sometimes confusion on the part of those you've contacted. The negative consequences of crossing hierarchical lines is potentially even worse: the ire of your superiors internally and offense on the part of those you've contacted, who might wonder why your organization has sent someone so junior to meet with them. Similarly, meeting with someone who is at the level of someone who works for you can deny that person an opportunity to establish and exercise that relationship and might diminish your status in the eyes of the person with whom you have requested the meeting.

If this all sounds a bit ridiculous in the context of modern American culture, where concerns about hierarchy are not terribly strong, keep in mind that we're talking about establishing professional relationships overseas. In many cultures -- especially traditional ones -- one's level and status play a much more important role in determining who can associate with whom. If you're not the senior person in your overseas operation, then you will want to know what those more senior than you prefer in this regard, as well as any strictures the local cultural dictates.

> **Lomé, Togo:** *When I was the ambassador in Togo, one of my officers invited me to dinner at her residence. When I arrived, I was surprised to find two government ministers among the guests. They were there because the officer knew them through her locally resident significant other. The problem was, Togo had just gone through yet another election marred by allegations of electoral fraud, and one of the ministers played a direct role in the conduct of the elections, about which I had complained to the government. Given our strained relations with the Togolese government on this point, I was managing my contact with the ministers – who in normal diplomatic practice are appropriately the ambassador's contacts – very strategically, so I was not pleased to find one of my officers amicably hosting them. I subsequently reminded my country team that contact with Togolese government ministers was my prerogative, and that where an officer required regular contact with a particular minister, we*

136

would meet with that minister together and establish that it was acceptable from the minister's perspective and mine for that officer to have direct contact. Diplomacy is serious stuff, and we don't want to send confusing signals.

The International Manager's Contacts

Now that we've discussed function and level, let's back away from the example of the UNDP HIV/AIDS program officer and talk about the relationships you would typically develop in your role as the person directly responsible for management of the overseas operation and its administrative platform, as opposed to one of its programs. As we've discussed before, depending on the size of your operation, you might be both its head and the person directly responsible for management issues and services. For our purposes here, however, we're going to focus on those contacts and relationships that are relevant to your management duties.

The nature of the country in which you're managing your overseas operation is going to have a big impact on who you need to know to get your job done. As we've already noted, the local culture has much to say about who can associate with whom, but there are other factors that affect this determination, as well. The country's level of development is principal among them. In a country where basic public utilities such as water and electricity are easily accessible and reliable, it might not be necessary for you to know senior people in the organizations that provide these services. You probably will need such contacts, however, in a country where underdeveloped or deteriorating infrastructure, or corruption, renders these services unreliable. Likewise with the goods and materials your organization needs to operate. In a country where cement, for instance, is readily available, you shouldn't need to know people who control or have access to cement supplies. If, however, you're building a new office compound in a country where the supply of cement is spotty and prone to shortages, you might be well served to befriend someone in the private sector or a government ministry who can pull the strings necessary to get you what you need.

Another major factor that is locally specific is the stability and reliability of the government and the services it provides, including safety and security. In countries where citizens demand and generally receive responsive services from their governments, you might not have to spend a lot of time cultivating relationships with a wide range of government officials that provide the services you need. Where, however, a country is poor and does not have the infrastructure it really requires to deliver a service, or where high levels of corruption affect how that service is delivered, you're going to need to know some key people.

Consistent with our belief that much of the growth in international management will continue to be in emerging and less developed countries, I'm going to assume that you will be managing an overseas operation in a country with an unreliable supply of goods and services, including government services. Thus, I'll suggest a full menu of professional contacts that you might draw from to develop your local network. We'll do this on a geographic basis, looking at relationships you need to cultivate with people at your organization's headquarters, people in the country where you are serving, and those in third countries who provide you goods, services, support or perhaps just good advice.

Relationships at Headquarters

During your first meeting, Tibor talked about the consultations that you need to undertake at headquarters before departing for your foreign assignment. This is the time to identify who, at headquarters, does what and specifically what support they can provide your overseas operation. Take the time to get to know them, and give them an opportunity to get to know you. Ask them to share with you their thoughts about the overseas operation. At this point, they can be more candid, because you bear no responsibility for what's happened there prior to your arrival. From where they sit, what are the most pressing problems at the overseas operation, and what do they think you should do about these problems once you arrive? I always learned a lot from sessions like this, and I found that, by asking questions and showing an interest in the views of a headquarters colleague, I had a more sympathetic person on the other end of the line when I had to call in from overseas for support.

So who is it important for the international manager to know at headquarters? That, of course, depends on the size and nature of your organization's headquarters. The U.S. Department of State, with over 250 overseas posts, has hundreds of people performing management functions, developing standard policies and procedures and providing administrative support to embassies and consulates around the world. Any of State's six regional bureaus is going to have at least four or five people just providing budget and fiscal support to posts in its regions, in addition to employees performing logistical, human resources and IT functions. An NGO with offices in 50 or 60 countries is going to have a much smaller number of people at headquarters backstopping its overseas operations administratively. In very small organizations, one headquarters employee might perform multiple management functions, such as financial and human resources support.

With that in mind, here's my list of people with whom you need to develop relationships at headquarters. If your headquarters doesn't have someone with the title I use in this list, it might at least have someone performing that function, so that's the person you'll need to get to know.

- The **budget and finance officer** or whoever determines how much money your operation receives. In my experience, these people like management officers who efficiently and effectively spend all of the money headquarters gives them. They obviously don't want you to spend more than you have, but they also don't want you to spend too little and then give it back to them – or worse, lose it – at the end of the fiscal year. A good relationship with your budget and fiscal officer at headquarters literally pays big dividends.

- The **post management officer** or **administrative liaison officer** responsible for tracking management issues at your operation and serving as your "utility infielder" at headquarters. In larger organizations, this person is the liaison between you, at your

140

overseas operation, and the large number of people who provide you administrative support from headquarters. Notice that, this important coordinating role aside, this position is second on my list *after* the budget and fiscal officer. My own strong preference is to have a direct relationship with the person or people who control my funding levels.

- The **executive director** responsible for *all* management related issues and support for operations in your part of the world (or perhaps the whole world in a smaller organization). This person's duties are usually so extensive that he or she will rarely have the opportunity to focus exclusively on your operation, unless there's some emergency – and that's exactly when you want them to recall their meeting with you and the positive impression you created.

- The **human resources officer** responsible for staffing expatriate positions at your operation and providing you guidance and support on other human resources issues. In large organizations, there might be a separate office that deals only with policies and compensation plans affecting your host country national (HCN) employees. If that's the case, you'll need to develop a good relationship with someone in that office, as well.

- The **real property officer** or the person responsible for tracking issues related to and providing funds for properties that the organization owns or leases at your overseas location. Some organizations rely principally on their people overseas to make decisions about the office and residential properties they need. Others with a large overseas presence and many properties have an office at headquarters that dictates policies with regard to the use, maintenance, renovation, leasing and construction of those properties. Where such an office exists, it often controls funds for the properties at your overseas operation, so it's important for you to have

141

supportive contacts in that office.

- The **program officer** or **desk officer** for the country in which your overseas office is located. Organizations do not exist to manage themselves; they manage themselves so that they can perform the functions and achieve the goals for which they do exist. This is also true of their overseas operations, which might be engaged in diplomacy, development assistance, or delivery of health, education or other services, etc. The program or desk officer is typically tracking and supporting the principal functions of the overseas operation and may or may not get involved in management issues and administrative support. Your reason for getting to know this person is to better understand the programs and activities you'll be supporting at the overseas operation and what headquarters' expectations are with regard to these programs and activities.

- The **information management officer** or **communications officer** responsible for supporting your overseas operation. Smaller organizations might not have anybody serving in this capacity at headquarters, which expects you to operate your IT and communications programs with locally available resources. Large organizations might have multiple offices performing IT and communications functions in support of your operation due to the presence of highly technical systems capable, perhaps, of processing classified information.

- Various **logistical support officers** who provide your overseas operation and expatriate employees assigned to it specific services and support. This is a broad category, which includes **shipping and transportation, procurement and contracting, and supply requisition**. An initial call on these offices prior to departing for post is a very good idea, because you can discuss problems that your operation might be having in connection with any specific service. Whether you maintain regular

142

contact with people providing these services or do so via your post management or administrative liaison officer depends on the size of management operations at headquarters and the problems you're experiencing at your operation overseas.

- The **medical officer** or the office responsible for establishing policies and providing medical support to your overseas operation. You want to know in general terms what your organization offers in this regard and who provides the support. It's particularly important to know whom to contact and how in the event of a medical emergency, especially if you're in a country that does not have adequate medical facilities and expertise locally available.

- The **security officer** responsible for supporting your overseas operation. Some operations overseas, such as U.S. embassies, have a security officer who does not report to the management officer. Security programs overseas tend to be resource intensive, however, and that means extensive support from the management office. So whether you will be directly responsible for security at the overseas operation or not, it's important to know about the security programs the organization has in place and any plans headquarters might have in this area for your overseas operation.

- **Management officers** at the headquarters of other agencies or divisions to which you provide management support at the overseas operation. If this is your situation, it's very useful to meet face-to-face with the people in those other headquarters who are responsible for ensuring that their people are getting what they need at your location. Support arrangements that reach across agencies or division, sometimes called shared services, can get tricky as other agencies or divisions complain that you're taking care of your own organization's people first, your costs are too high, or you're not providing good service. Introducing yourself to these people,

143

explaining your philosophy about shared services (which, one hopes, includes a strong dose of equity in service delivery), and inviting them to contact you directly if they have any questions or problems can help to reduce tensions that naturally occur in shared service systems.

Relationships with People in Third Countries

Some organizations have regional offices that provide support of various types to the organization's overseas operations in their region. Perhaps your operation doesn't have a resident budget and fiscal officer. You perform budget and fiscal tasks yourself, but you might receive support from a regional budget and fiscal officer, who is not only available by phone or e-mail, but who makes periodic visits to provide more comprehensive service. There might likewise be a regional human resources officer, security officer, or medical officer. You want to find out who and where these people are and establish contact with them before or soon after you arrive at your overseas assignment. My practice was to invite these people to pay a visit to my operation as soon as possible after my arrival. When they came, I would not only give them as much of my time and attention as possible, but would also try to show them a good time after hours so that they considered a trip to my location an enjoyable experience and looked forward to coming back.

Regional support aside, the other people you want to get to know in third countries are your counterparts in the region: the management officers at your organization's operations in neighboring and nearby countries. It's extremely useful to be able to compare notes with these people and seek their advice. Very often, their experiences will be similar to yours, and they will often have good ideas for addressing some of the challenges you're facing. Sometimes, they will even be in a position to provide concrete support.

Addis Ababa, Ethiopia*: When I arrived in Addis Ababa as the U.S. Embassy's management officer*

*in 1988, I found a warehouse almost literally overflowing
with new stoves, washers and dryers. What's more, the
appliances in our residential quarters were also new. I
found out that the management section had ordered all of
these appliances at the end of the previous fiscal year to
spend money that would otherwise be returned to the U.S.
Treasury, if left unspent. Now we had a warehouse
crammed with enough appliances to replace all of the new
appliances in our residences, when in fact what we
needed was perhaps two or three of each type of
appliance in reserve. I sent a message around to the
management officers at the U.S. embassies in neighboring
countries asking them if they cared to have any of these
surplus appliances for the cost of shipping. A few of my
counterparts jumped on the offer, and within a few
months, I had enough space to organize my warehouse
properly.*

It's not uncommon for organizations to hold regional
conferences for the management officers of their operations in a
region. Such occasions provide an excellent opportunity to
compare notes and develop useful relationships with your
colleagues.

Relationships in Country

We've already discussed how your function (in this case,
as management officer) and your level in the organization affect
the relationships that you will need to establish to perform your
duties effectively. But who do you really need to know? Let's
consider your potential universe of contacts in country. It's
useful to keep these categories of contacts in mind as you
approach any particular management issue and consider to
whom you might reach out:

- **Host country officials:** Many of the management
  issues that affect your overseas operation will in some
  way involve the host government. The issue at hand
  will determine which official you need to reach out to,
  but there will be some officials with whom you are in

145

regular contact, and you will want to cultivate a good working relationship with these individuals. Here's an illustrative rather than exhaustive list of host government offices within which you might want to have a close contact:

o The **Chief of Protocol's Office** in the Ministry of Foreign Affairs: This office is typically responsible for determining the status of foreign organizations and individuals in country (including your operation's expatriate employees) and what that status implies about any privileges or immunities they might enjoy or special obligations they might have.

o **Immigration**: A good contact in Immigration can be useful if working level immigration officials challenge the status of one of your expatriate employees or their family members either arriving in or departing the country.

o **Customs:** Your operation will almost certainly bring in shipments from headquarters and elsewhere, to include the household effects of your expatriate employees. As things come in, you will want to clear them through Customs as quickly as possible. Unfortunately, in many countries, Customs is an easy place for papers to get "lost" and shipments stuck. It is often also prone to corruption. Having a good contact there can yield immediate practical results.

o **Ministry of Finance:** This Ministry deals with issues of currency exchange and transfer, as well as taxation. The latter issue will affect, at a minimum, your HCN employees, the reporting of their income, whether your organization must withdraw taxes on their behalf, etc. A good contact there might also be in a position to provide you information about the state of the economy and host government actions in that

146

connection that could have an effect on your organization.

o **Interior Ministry:** Unlike the U.S. Department of the Interior, other countries' Interior Ministries generally have authority over the police and other security services. An Interior Ministry contact will not only be useful if your organization requires special protection for some reason, but also in the event that lower level security personnel cause problems for members of your operation's staff – expatriate or HCN.

o **Ministry of Labor:** Employment of HCN staff will be governed by host country labor laws, some provisions of which might also apply to your operation's expatriate staff. Foreign organizations often have awkward relations with labor ministries because they're square pegs trying to fit into round holes. Identifying and cultivating a sympathetic contact in the Ministry of Labor can keep your operation out of trouble.

o **Ministry of Health:** The utility of contacts in the Ministry of Health will depend on the extent to which the Ministry controls your access to the medical services, medications and supplies your operation requires. Well informed contacts in this Ministry can also provide you useful information about developing health conditions that affect your operation.

o **Ministry of Telecommunications:** If your operational requirements for telecommunication services are out of the ordinary or you are unable to satisfy them easily, you could well require the assistance of someone senior in this Ministry to make things happen. The need to operate your own telecommunication system or emergency radio network will almost certainly argue in favor of cultivating such a relationship.

147

- **Non-Governmental Host Country Contacts:** A wide range of host country organizations and individuals provide goods, services or information that you will require to manage your operation. These sources could be from the private or nonprofit sectors:

  - **Health care providers:** As I mentioned during our meeting on the care and feeding of expatriate employees, the overseas operation will typically bear some responsibility for the health of these individuals and their families. You need to ensure that any local medical services your section arranges meet your organization's standards. Developing mutually supportive, perhaps even formal, relationships with competent local health care providers will give you peace of mind in this regard.

  - **Vendors and service providers:** As management officer, it's unlikely that you'll be running around making purchases and lining up services yourself. Your HCN staff will generally do that. There might be, however, vendors of things that are in short, unpredictable supply or providers of critical services that are worth getting to know personally, so that, in a pinch you can reach out and obtain what your organization needs. It's hard to say exactly who these individuals might be or which goods and service they might represent, but it was from experience rather than coincidence that, earlier in this meeting, I mentioned those who have some control over cement supplies. Reliable access to building supplies can often be an issue in poorer countries, and having someone who can deliver what you need can spare you aggravating and costly delays on important construction projects. In the places I have served as a management officer, I have also established a good working relationship with the individual running the

148

company that provided travel services for my operation. There have been many times when I needed someone who could pull strings on very short notice to get a staff member on a flight, often in a medical emergency or due to a death in the employee's family.

- o **Legal services:** Inevitably, your operation will require the services of a local attorney to deal with a specific problem or situation. It's not unusual for the management officer to bear responsibility for managing legal issues as they arise, so a good working relationship with this local attorney can be very useful. In fact, if you have found someone effective and trustworthy in this regard, it might be useful to keep that person on retainer.

- o **Banking services:** Good relations with officials at the local bank where your organization has its accounts can be very important in countries where the currency is not convertible and there are tight restrictions on the transfer of funds between headquarters and your operation.

- **Embassy or Consulate Officials:** Here, I'm referring to diplomatic and consular officials of the country you and the expatriate staff of your overseas operation come from or the country with which your organization is identified. If you work for an international organization, in fact, your operation won't be identified with any particular embassy.

Their diplomatic functions aside, embassies and their consulates bear some responsibility for the safety and wellbeing of their citizens in country. Their consular sections normally offer a wide range of services from passport issuance to limited assistance in the case of arrest, theft or death. In the case of U.S. embassies and consulates, the consular section operates a "warden system" through which it alerts Americans of

149

emergencies and other situations that require their attention. If you're managing something other than an embassy or consulate, I would strongly recommend developing a good relationship with officers at the nearest consular section and ensuring that your expatriate employees have registered their presence in country with the appropriate consular section.

In addition to consular services, more robust diplomatic services, like that of the United States, provide other information and services that will be of interest to you and your expatriate staff. It's common for American ambassadors to hold periodic town hall meetings with locally resident citizens to share information and views about what's going on in country. Commercial sections can be useful sources of information about import and export procedures and regulations. Security officers are generally pleased to share assessments of the local security situation and provide advice on precautionary measures.

Knowing what support or guidance your country's embassy is able to offer and cultivating relationships with the relevant embassy or consulate officials can be of great benefit to you. As the management officer of an overseas operation, I would definitely want to develop a good relationship with the management officer of my country's embassy or consulate early in my tenure. Embassies and consulates have often been in country a long time and have a lot of experience and advice their officials are willing to share about some of the management challenges that confront you.

- **The Expatriate Community and Expatriate Organizations:** The expatriate community in general is a useful source of information on a wide range of issues, both professional and related to lifestyle. There are, in fact, some expatriate organizations and

150

groups that will be of particular use to you in executing your management responsibilities:

- **American Chamber of Commerce (sometimes called AmCham):** Member run, AmCham is, among other things, a forum for discussing a wide range of issues, including management issues, affecting American businesses and organizations in country.

- **Overseas Security Advisory Council (OSAC):** Run under the aegis of the U.S. Department of State, and convened by the Regional Security Officer of the U.S. Embassy, OSAC provides resident American organizations information about the security situation in country and a forum for discussing appropriate safety measures and actions.

- **International school:** We spoke previously about the importance of supporting the international school or schools which most of your expatriate employees' children attend. In addition to supporting an international school on behalf of your expatriate staff, you might find that it faces some of the same management challenges that you are grappling with and might have useful advice to share.

- **Management officers at other foreign organizations:** Just as it can be very useful to be in contact with your own organization's management officers elsewhere in the region, it can also be beneficial to know the management officers of other foreign organizations in country. They are very likely dealing with many of the same management issues that affect your work. My standard practice, as an embassy management officer, was to contact the management officers of other embassies in country soon after my arrival. If there wasn't

151

already an established group, I would invite these management officers collectively to my house for lunch and then get them to agree to host a monthly lunch on a rotating basis. The lunches provided both a forum for sharing management information and an opportunity to develop social bonds.

I hope that this meeting has stimulated some good ideas about the relationships you would like to cultivate at headquarters, in third countries, and most importantly, in your country of assignment. As I said before, your professional network is going to depend, to a significant degree, on the nature of the country in which you're serving and the management problems that confront you. The broad categories of contacts we identified, however, should serve as a useful guide for nearly any overseas management assignment.

2:30 p.m.   ***Meeting with Ambassador Nagy***
                                    Safety and Security – Job one

"Tibor – you're Duty Officer, right? My house is under attack by armed robbers – can you do something, please?"

---US Embassy, Lusaka employee to one of the authors at 2:00 a.m. on the emergency radio

Lagos, Nigeria: *With poverty, political turmoil, economic collapse, failing infrastructure, a lack of sanitation, shocking traffic jams, and rampant crime, Lagos was one of the most unlivable cities on earth. Our embassy's policy was that all American employees had to travel between the city and its distant airport – a trip which could take anywhere from two to five hours – in a partially armored SUV with a driver. One employee chaffed at this policy, believing that it was an affront to his personal freedom, and decided to ignore it. On the day he was driving to the airport with his family to go on vacation, traffic was especially bad, and neighborhood gang members, called "area boys", used the opportunity to rob drivers in the stalled vehicles. Without the protection offered by armoring, our employee's vehicle was an obvious and easy target and was quickly surrounded. In addition to stealing all of his belongings and terrorizing his family, the area boys badly cut the unfortunate employee with their machetes; he spent his vacation recovering in a European hospital rather than taking well-earned R&R.*

153

After this incident there were no more grumblings about "unreasonable" security requirements: everyone on staff dutifully took the armored cars to and from the airport, and no one else was hurt.

Today's international manager is much more likely to be posted to Lagos, Nigeria (recently called the world's most dangerous city) than London or Geneva. Instead of worrying about what cultural event to attend next weekend, your employees will more likely be concerned about crime, political insecurity, diseases, lack of water and electricity, where to buy gasoline, and similar life-impacting factors. My intention for this meeting is to help you prepare for the day-to-day dangers to health, safety and security which cannot be avoided – they will be part of your environment. In the next session, Greg will discuss how to deal with bona fide crises. While some are clearly unavoidable, I do hope that by careful planning and threat avoidance we can keep you from crossing the crisis line and having to implement his excellent advice! Remember, you have many goals and priorities, but nothing is more important than keeping your staff as safe and secure as possible. I've divided our discussions by categories, starting with the most common – issues which you'll likely face, and ending with those that few will ever have to worry over.

Before we begin, here are a few general comments. While each locale is unique, in much of the world the categories below will impact day-to-day life to some extent. Of course, their relative importance will differ, and may even change during your posting. For instance, a bad election can immediately move "political violence" to the top over "dangerous traffic". The key to keeping your staff safe and well is to continually assess current conditions, and to be aware of special events coming down the line such as general strikes, elections, religious demonstrations, significant anniversaries, etc. (See my previous comments on the usefulness of local employees for such awareness.) The following tools will be greatly useful in your safety/security oversight:

- **Emergency Action Plan (EAP).** In the next meeting, Greg will discuss the usefulness of an EAP in

154

addressing crisis situations. While the document is geared towards managing crises, a section of the EAP should be focused on dealing with common emergencies - medical; criminal; utility; traffic – based on local circumstances, and complete with current contact information and directions to key places, such as health clinic, police station, hospital, etc. When your kitchen is on fire, or your child swallows poison is not the time to figure out whether there is a functioning fire department or ambulance service!

- **Enforcing Policies Related to Safety/Security Concerns.** The incident above illustrates why certain uniform safety/security policies are absolutely required. Your local circumstances will no doubt warrant others. Such policies are useless if they are ignored by the staff, and unenforced by the leadership. Reasons for non-compliance can vary from a policy being seen, rightly or wrongly, as unnecessary, to employee bravado. In any case, it is imperative for management to set those policies which are necessary, to explain them to the community affected, and then to monitor compliance and punish "refuseniks". This can vary from a mild reprimand to expulsion from post, based on seriousness of policy being flaunted.

Addis Ababa, Ethiopia: Due to the incredibly high rate of motor vehicle accidents, plus the unbelievably unsafe driving conditions on rural roads, including dilapidated road surfaces, vehicles parked on the road, animals on the road, people sleeping on the road, large vehicles passing at any point with total disregard for oncoming traffic, vehicles not using lights, etc., we had a policy against anyone driving outside the city at night. A group of senior employees – experienced with local conditions – was trying to get away for a weekend visit to a distant game park. Their departure was delayed due to some last minute work requirements, so – against my better judgment – I authorized them to leave, knowing that they

155

would have to drive several hours in darkness. My fears were realize when, shortly after dark, we received a radio message that they had run into a parked bus and urgently needed help. To compound my mistake, I sent our very experienced and cautious motor pool supervisor to go help them. Unfortunately, shortly outside the city he ran into a herd of cattle, destroying his vehicle. Thankfully no one was seriously hurt, but my misplaced good intentions resulted in the loss of two brand new, high cost vehicles. I never again allowed any deviation from established driving policies!

- **Contingency Planning**. As I noted above, assessing current conditions and being aware of special upcoming events is the best way to keep your community safe. Of course, you must do something with that information. It's a delicate balance between keeping your community informed and alert, and causing people to panic, or being accused of constantly "crying wolf." Many African cities, for example, have a high level of property crime and theft at the best of times – but the period immediately preceding a major holiday suffers an additional "bump" in criminal activity. It is totally appropriate to remind employees of this fact when a holiday approaches, and revisit common sense procedures to avoid being victimized. Weekly notices, however, written in alarmist language about rampant crime, are not helpful.

- **Tripwires, or keeping the frog from boiling.** In some locales there may be one or two factors which affect your overall safety and security, while in others, everything is amiss. We used to wryly joke, for example, that two weeks in Lagos was like three years anywhere else, when it came to unpleasant incidents. If your post veers towards the latter type, you and your staff have to make sure you know when the overall situation passes from the "normal" to the "time to start sending folks home" phase. The best way to prepare for this is to establish in advance clear "trip wires" which will alert you that day-to-day life has entered a new, more risky stage where you have to re-evaluate your level of staffing and operations. It sounds blasé, but human beings are incredibly adaptable, and what may seem incredibly abnormal and dangerous one day, quickly becomes routine. With "trip wires" you can avoid being the frog which never realizes how hot the water is getting until it is boiled!

Yaounde, Cameroon: The 1993 elections went very badly and the incumbent president clearly stole the victory. The population expressed its outrage through a series of "villes mortes" (Ghost Town) campaigns – using general strikes and mob violence to close all commerce, industry, and circulation in towns and cities. When the campaign started, our embassy established events (trip wires) which would result in our ambassador reducing the staff, sending dependents home, and recommending that all U.S. citizens leave Cameroon. In retrospect I'm relieved that we did – since we all became quite used to angry crowds stoning vehicles which were out and about (you learned to make quick U-turns). The international school students joked about having to quickly enter their buildings when a police helicopter swooped overhead daily to drop tear gas on the university campus next door. Such events went on for several months, and although none of the wires were "tripped," without them in place we would never have noticed that the water was getting hot!

Unhealthful Conditions

Some type of health problem will affect almost everyone who spends more than a few weeks in a new locale, ranging in severity from mild stomach upsets to death due to an environmental hazard, such as poisonous snakes or unexploded land mines. Some brief examples below will illustrate the great range of health dangers:

- *An embassy employee in northern Togo was bitten by a scorpion while visiting a game park. The local doctor told him, "You will either die within three hours, or your body will tolerate the poison and nothing much will happen." He spent a nerve wracking three hours, but was fine thereafter.*

- *Two Peace Corps Volunteers in rural Cameroon suffered serious injuries when their bush taxi drove off the road. They were brought by chartered aircraft to the capital, where embassy employees gave blood (since the local supply was unsafe due to HIV concerns), so they could be stabilized. They were airlifted by air ambulance to Switzerland and recovered.*

- *Two Peace Corps Volunteers in Togo were attacked by thousands of bees while riding their motor scooters – suffering countless stings. Local residents had to light fires to drive off the bees before they could take the volunteers to a clinic. Unfortunately it was too late, and the clinic did not have the proper medication, so the volunteers died.*

- *A U.S. government employee at a high-altitude African post continued playing tennis despite feeling chest pains and suffered a fatal heart attack hours after stopping. Local medical facilities could not help him.*

- *Two young sons of missionaries working in Cameroon developed high fevers shortly after arriving for home leave in Canada. Despite immediate and modern medical intervention, the two died within days. Cause of death was found to be cerebral malaria, something Canadian doctors never even considered.*

- *The infant child of an NGO country representative in Ethiopia drank a full bottle of malaria preventative medicine. Luckily the parents discovered it in time,*

158

and, by our quickly authorizing treatment by the embassy health unit, the child was saved.

The examples go on and on. The key point is to prepare: do a thorough evaluation of conditions at post, determine what are the most common health issues that can impact your staff, and identify available remedies and resources for addressing the risks. Your "welcome to post" guide should fully address all of the major health concerns, and the residential "welcome kits" should be stocked with health related items. Following is a general guide:

- Trauma kit

- Iodine tablets for cleaning water

- Information on what local foods are safe and unsafe, and food/water preparation guide

- Instructions on where competent medical help is available

- Information on quality of locally available drugs and sources

- Instructions on what to do in case of medical emergency

- Information on local maladies with symptoms and treatment

On arrival, employees need a thorough health/medical orientation, along with information on other safety/security issues. Make sure your employees actually travel the route from their residence to the closest adequate medical facility – the time to try is not late at night in the midst of an emergency. Also, if you are in a country where you routinely evacuate serious medical cases, make sure your staff knows how to initiate the process. I can assure you from experience, the most urgent cases will arise at the most inconvenient times – so be prepared!

Other Health Issues: Based on your location, HIV/AIDS, substance abuse, and mental health issues may be major concerns for your operations. In parts of Sub-Saharan Africa,

159

the HIV infection rate exceeds 30 percent - so your folks should be aware of the dangers. If you are in a place without support for employees struggling with addiction issues, don't let them come. I had someone assigned to one of my posts who had been through an alcohol treatment program three times – and there was no AA chapter at post. The result was a disaster – for the employee and the post! If you are in a place without counseling facilities, and have employees going through serious relationship or personal problems, send them away. Your decisive leadership will likely prevent domestic violence or even suicide; it's in their interest, your interest, and the organization's interest.

Travel Safety

The greatest single safety concern at all of my postings was over traffic and travel. Driving conditions, driving culture, emergency response capabilities, and safety standards all vary enormously – and are usually much worse than in the U.S. Again, to get a sense of the scope of the threats, here are a few examples:

160

- *After a 1993 visit by the FAA to the Lagos International Airport (Nigeria), it was declared unsafe; official U.S. government travelers had the option to use Cotonou airport in neighboring Benin, a four to five hour drive. Those who did so were wise, as Lagos suffered a series of fatal aircraft accidents in subsequent years – including a crash landing which was totally survivable. The crew immediately vacated the aircraft, as panicked passengers tried to retrieve their belongings and blocked off the exits. There was no response from airport authorities for hours; the aircraft caught fire after about twenty minutes and most passengers died.*

- *A Washington based employee in Naples on a short visit decided to take a lunch time stroll on his first day. Leaving the consulate building, he waited for the traffic signal at the corner to change to show that pedestrians could cross, and he stepped into the street. He was immediately hit by a vehicle and died shortly thereafter. He had not realized that in much of the world, a red light is nothing more than a suggestion for motorists to be vigilant.*

- *A car full of embassy employees and Washington visitors was touring refugee areas in rural Guinea when the driver overturned the car while trying to avoid an especially deep pothole. Passers-by took our seriously injured employees to a near-by health clinic – which, like most rural African health facilities, was woefully short of medication and supplies. Luckily, embassy policy required all official vehicles to be equipped with two first aid kits, including one for major trauma. The clinic staff was able to save everyone by using the supplies in the kits, and we were able to air evacuate the injured to Abidjan, Côte d'Ivoire (the closest city with adequate medical facilities).*

- *Driving away with my family from the embassy's weekend campground in rural Ethiopia, I had the misfortune of hitting a goat in one of the small towns on the road back to Addis Ababa. A large, hostile crowd started to gather. Thinking quickly, I realized that I would have to pay an enormous sum – not only for the value of the goat (which no doubt was the prize of the herd), but also for any progeny it might have produced, along with the progeny of the progeny. I quickly drove off – with the angry crowd raising fists and throwing rocks.*

The above examples illustrate the variety of travel dangers and, again, highlight the importance of staying up to date with local conditions and properly orienting new arrivals. In developing countries especially, travel conditions can change incredibly fast: roads collapse, previously safe areas become dangerous, the airline with the new planes everyone trusted loses its only experienced pilot, the only ferry connecting two strategic points sinks, etc. Make sure you keep your travel policies up to date to reflect current conditions, and enforce them for the welfare of all. If you require that your organization's employees use a local driver to visit certain parts of the country, and someone fails to do so – take quick and decisive action. Otherwise everyone will suffer when a tragedy occurs!

Environmental Safety

Lusaka, Zambia: My first job as a diplomat included overseeing our maintenance services. Since there were no local contractors who could perform up to U.S. standards, the embassy maintained its own plumbers, electricians, casual workers, etc. My first day on the job, I visited a work site where our employees were remodeling a kitchen in an embassy residence. Getting out of the car, the first thing I saw was our electrician standing on the top of a rickety ladder, without safety glasses or helmet, electric drill in hand, trailing a cord plugged into a long, stripped extension, laying in a large pool of water. Looking further at the job site I saw carpenters handling power saws without the slightest concern for safety, painters using cleaning chemicals which constituted a serious fire danger, and on and on...

162

    While parts of Western Europe are even stricter about environmental safety than the U.S., most countries are lax to the extent that your employees' health and safety is seriously jeopardized. Whether it is unsafe pesticides, counterfeit products, or defective electrical wiring, you need to be aware of risks to your staff from products and services that rarely cause concern in the U.S., although Americans are becoming more sensitized to this problem after a series of publicized incidents concerning health risks from certain Chinese manufactured products. In much of the world, it's much better to assume that a product is unsafe, or that a contractor will try and install a defective part, or that the wiring is substandard – rather than believing that all is well. This, again, is where experienced and trusted local employees are crucial to your operations – they know local practices but also understand your expectations and standards. Despite the vignette I presented above, I was able – through the carrot and stick approach and much patience – to instill a working environment which focused on safety and thoroughness. Whether or not my Zambian employees ever valued this, or even if my standards survived my departure, was not my concern – I believed it was important to our operations. As the manager, you can set the standards when it comes to environmental safety. Not doing so can have tragic consequences. One of my colleagues in Yaounde had almost burned to death while posted to Ndjamena, Chad. Because of shoddy workmanship, his air conditioning wires overheated in the ceiling and started a slow burning fire. After reaching a critical temperature, the flames erupted simultaneously all over the house – trapping him inside behind his burglar bars and steel door. Thanks only to his quick thinking security guard – who used an axe to break open the door – did he escape death.

Crime

> *Lusaka, Zambia: In the late 70s and early 80s Lusaka was one of the most crime ridden cities on earth. Heavily armed rebels who were trying to overthrow the regime in neighboring Rhodesia were based in the city and often participated in home invasions, rapes, and other violent crimes. The local police, understaffed, under armed and unmotivated, were useless – never having transport available to go to a crime scene. One night when I was duty officer, I was called on the embassy emergency radio by a distraught staff member whose house was in the process of being broken into by an armed gang. Grabbing the submachine gun I kept under the bed, I first drove to a police station and persuaded the two officers on duty to come with me to my colleague's house. Arriving at the scene, the two police refused to leave the vehicle until I did. When I exited the car, they did so as well – reluctantly – and immediately fired their WWII vintage single shot Enfield's into the air. I said, "That will make the robbers run away," and one of them replied, "Yes, we hope so." Going around the side of the house, ablaze with night lights, I pointed out a darkened area, saying, "That's where the robbers may be hiding." They agreed, and one of them suggested that I go check it out. Fortunately the gang must have left when we drove up, but these types of home invasions were commonplace and our community was in great angst for many years.*

Sadly, the above situation is not uncommon in the developing world, or even in some middle income countries (e.g., Brazil, South Africa). Crime can fit into the threat category I described earlier where it's critically important for the manager to not only have a realistic sense of current conditions, but also to know where trends are headed. If residential robberies are on the increase, you should get headquarter's approval now for 24 hour protection for your houses, not after the first incident. Greg cites a great organization to help with crises planning – the Department of State's Overseas Security Advisory Council (www.osac.gov). They are equally useful in providing information on crime worldwide, and they organize an annual conference in Washington to brief OSAC members on global trends. This is another area where it is essential that the new arrivals' guide and face-to face orientation provide complete, up to date information describing local conditions, ways to avoid being a victim, and how to get help. Here are some other items to consider:

- Host government capabilities, competence, responsiveness, corruption.

- Availability of private security companies. Are they efficient, responsive, and professional? If not, can you create your own private security force?

- A weapons policy for your employees and security personnel. If you permit either your staff or private guards to keep weapons, you will need to have a "use of lethal force" policy.

East Africa. *Armed robbers attacked an embassy residence in the middle of the night. The U.S. diplomat who lived there had an unregistered shotgun, which he first discharged into the air. When the robbers kept up their effort to break down the door, he stood ready and fired at close range when they broke through – killing two, while the others ran away. When the police finally arrived, they congratulated him – remarking that the two dead robbers were well known criminals -- and they*

165

pulled the bodies into the house – since local law allowed a homeowner to use deadly force if, and only if, the intruders were completely within the premises. The local government never said a word about the incident.

- Written minimum standards for security at all staff housing, including perimeter fencing, outside lights, solid core doors, alarm system with panic buttons, safe haven (panic room), emergency communications equipment, window grills, etc., are all items to be considered.

- Partially armored, or fully armored vehicles for moving staff and accompanying family members between vulnerable areas.

- Written policies and procedures for your locale: no-go areas, travel, curfews, emergency contacts, known criminal practices, reporting cases of unusual interest in buildings, people, etc., need to be addressed.

- Other places which the staff frequent, such as international schools, clubs, and other local attractions, should be included in your security policy.

Beyond providing physical impediments to crime, you must impart to your staff that personal security is an awareness and an attitude. Whether your local concerns are carjackings, home invasions, kidnappings, scams, rapes, whatever – the unpleasant truth is that the best way for your folks to stay safe is to make sure they are the most difficult targets in the community. It's not that you want the bad guys to go after the neighboring residences, offices, cars, etc. – you just want to keep your community safe!

In addition to providing the most crime free environment possible, you also have to make sure you plan for the "what if" contingencies. The person on your staff responsible for security should establish excellent personal rapport with key officials in the local security services before anything happens. Everyone should know where to go for medical treatment (see above); and you should be prepared to send traumatized employees out of the country for counseling if there are no resources at your post. Crime will become a greater and greater menace as urban populations grow along with more limited opportunities for the millions of young men seeking economic advancement. Be prepared!

Hostile Intelligence

Whether it's the local government, your competitors, or even criminal gangs, there may be people out to steal your secrets. Here again, local conditions and capabilities vary widely, and you need to decide whether your response to such activities will be active or passive. At a minimum, you will need to brief your incoming staff on who is after what, the methods they are using (technical or human) to gain information, what your policies are regarding the protection of information and how your organization is responding to such attempts. You can be fairly certain that among your locally recruited staff there will likely be individuals who are being paid by someone else to provide information on you, your operations, your habits, your families, etc., to steal documents or other materials, or to place technical eavesdropping equipment on your premises, vehicles, etc. At my various postings this was always the case: sometimes we knew who was doing what, sometimes we suspected, and sometimes we had no idea. Your response will depend on the egregiousness of the activity, your relations with the host government, the value of the employee(s) involved, and similar considerations. I have been in situations where it was useful to have an "earpiece" for the local government. For example if my driver was reporting overheard conversations, we could selectively feed information (or misinformation) at our option. On the other hand, if I discovered that the local accountant or telecommunications tech was also on someone else's payroll, I usually got rid of them since they could do considerable damage to the operations. Again, conditions and responses vary greatly, but it's definitely a security threat which you have to seriously consider.

Political Violence and General Insecurity:

> *Conakry, Guinea: The Guinean opposition refused to accept the results of the 1998 elections which returned President Conte to another term with a large majority. Unfortunately, the voting was split among ethnic lines and inter-ethnic tensions in the capital boiled over into sporadic violence. The opposition also organized daily demonstrations which resulted in crowds burning tires, stoning vehicles, and closing off large sections of Conakry. I had to decide whether the risks were such that we should start sending our family members, and perhaps some employees out – or whether the situation would calm down. While the initial outrage against the election results was intense, and some members of the embassy were concerned that the situation would explode, my feeling, based on discussions with government and opposition figures, was that conditions would gradually improve. I decided on a "wait and see" posture for the next two days – closing the embassy and asking our staff to stay home. Indeed the violence decreased and Conakry returned to "normal" within the week. It was a close call – but the right one: I believed that it was more dangerous to try and move people around at the height of the chaos; if things got worse, we'd have to get them out anyway, but it was worth staying put for a while.*

Some places are generally unstable, while others experience periods of chaos due to special circumstances, such as elections, ethnic or religious frictions, etc. Your challenge here is to avoid becoming the frog in the boiling water, and having your situation deteriorate into the "crises" categories Greg will discuss in your next meeting, without you having taken appropriate action, e.g., getting your folks out! In some respects, it's more difficult to evaluate situations which are consistently dangerous – how do you decide that a trip wire has been activated when driving anywhere at any time or doing just about anything has an element of risk? This is the type of environment where consultations with other international organizations and businesses are essential. The local OSAC council, if there is

168

one, is a great source for consolidated data showing types and numbers of incidents; from it you can get a good sense of overall trends. In such situations I have found organizational culture greatly impacts how they deal with the dangers. There are some used to dealing with really dangerous places, and these are quite blasé about local circumstances. Others, new to such places, ("This never happened in Geneva!") have quite the opposite reaction. Your job is to be objective: never dismiss threats to your folks, but don't over-react. Planning ahead and establishing trip wires in an objective setting, will really help when chaos erupts.

Terrorism

Terrorist incidents have now occurred nearly everywhere, undertaken by groups holding grievances over religion, politics, ethnicity, environmental concerns, economics, culture, etc. Regardless of the cause behind the bomb, innocents are still killed and maimed. Of course, some places are more vulnerable than others; currently, for example, Baghdad and Kabul, and some organizations (just about any building sporting an Israeli or American flag) are targeted more often. Risks vary, but no one, anywhere is totally safe. As with the other security and safety factors I discussed above, your posture will be based on local conditions and you will know your vulnerabilities, risks, likely terrorists, etc. There are, however, some general principles which are helpful in keeping your staff safe:

- Act on any situation or person which sends warning signs. For example, there is something intuitively wrong with a man riding a bus while dressed in an overcoat on a hot summer day, or someone leaving a backpack on a train and getting off.

- If your "radar" tells you something is wrong, it likely is. Act – don't hesitate. It's much better to be embarrassed by jumping off a bus or directing a conductor to a package than being blown to bits.

169

- Conduct "intruder" and "bomb" drills in your organization. Anyone regularly answering a phone should have a report form available in case there is a telephone threat (e.g., bomb, kidnapping). This makes sure everyone responds the same way, asks for valuable information, etc. Make sure everyone knows ahead of time what to do in each of the above situations.

- Depending on the threat level, thoroughly check every vehicle entering your facility. Make no exceptions – especially for the "boss" – otherwise it loses all credibility.

- Make sure physical impediments to vehicle bombs are in place around your building, and that personal entry, exit controls and movement controls within your facility adhere to threat levels.

- Terrorist incidents often come in multiples and can be timed to maximize casualties; the secondary vehicle explodes just as emergency responders arrive to help victims of the first. Many of our American Embassy colleagues in Nairobi were killed or injured when terrorists attacked the embassy in August 1998 because they went to their windows immediately after the first, smaller explosion went off, just when the larger bomb exploded, shredding them with glass. Your folks should know to stay away when they hear an explosion, gunfire, etc.

The Clash of Cultures:

Lagos, Nigeria: When I was posted to Nigeria in the mid-90s, the Netherlands Embassy sent a deputy ambassador who was gay and came accompanied by his partner. They did their best to conduct their social life as they would have in Amsterdam, and the diplomatic community did its best to be supportive. Unfortunately, their lifestyle raised intense hostility from Nigerian officialdom and society. One evening, just outside their home, they were beset by a gang of local toughs and savagely beaten. It was not for their money, but simply because of who they were. They departed shortly thereafter.

Governments and businesses have faced this difficult decision for decades when sending representatives to other nations who faced hostility because of their sex, color, religion, or lifestyle. The dilemma has been to what extent we compromise what we stand for as an equal opportunity society, versus how sending a certain person will impact our objectives in the mission, or even threaten our representative's safety. Missionaries have been struggling with this issue for centuries; many have lost their lives, and some continue to do so. While not as life-threatening, President Reagan sending the first African-American ambassador to then-apartheid South Africa (Edward Perkins) was just as dramatic and certainly presented some threats to Ambassador Perkins' safety. But both the president and Ambassador Perkins were eager to show apartheid South Africa that U.S. society used the talents of all of our citizens in all capacities, including the most senior. And Ambassador Perkins went on to play a significant role in mediating an end to apartheid. As an international manager, you have to carefully weigh how you can comply with the letter and spirit of U.S. non-discrimination laws, while knowing the types of difficulties certain persons will face at your post because of cultural factors or even laws (e.g., women not being allowed to drive in Saudi Arabia). Make sure the information material at your headquarters about such factors is complete and accurate – so that when your headquarters HR department makes personnel assignments to your post, such factors are fully considered – and neither the person assigned, nor your company, will be going into such a posting with blinders. In addition, once such an assignment is made, you will have to carefully consider the safety/security implications, and will have to make whatever additional accommodations are necessary to provide for the new arrival's well-being.

Final Thoughts

If you take nothing more away from this session, please remember the following: know what's going on related to safety/security conditions at your post city and country; know of special circumstances which may be on the horizon which will impact your security; plan for contingencies – including the all-important "trip wires" which will induce you to take certain pre-determined actions; establish, communicate and enforce policies based on what you know; prepare and keep up-to-date, instructional material for all of your staff; and thoroughly brief all new arrivals and their family members on how to stay safe and secure.

For myself, during my long diplomatic career within the communities which were my responsibility, I lost one colleague to a vehicle accident, another to suicide, and two Peace Corps volunteers to bee stings. But I am relieved to know that our vigilance and pro-active approach resulted in many lives saved and injuries prevented. Please do even better!

3:15 p.m.

Meeting with Ambassador Engle
When Crisis Strikes

*Great emergencies and crises show us how much
greater our vital resources [physical, intellectual and
moral] are than we had supposed.*

---William James

Addis Ababa, Ethiopia: *As I disembarked from the flight
back from summer vacation, the embassy expeditor gave
me the news that a small plane carrying Texas
Congressman Mickey Leland's delegation, five embassy
colleagues and several Ethiopian officials had not
returned from a trip to a refugee camp upcountry. It was,
as we spoke, many hours late, and the embassy had
learned that it never arrived at the camp earlier in the
day. The next two weeks, in addition to being gut
wrenchingly sad, were without a doubt the busiest and
most intense I have ever experienced. ALL other work
was pushed aside as the embassy, the U.S. military, a
State Department task force, and the Ethiopian
government did everything possible to find the aircraft,
and then, sadly, recover the bodies of the 19 victims of the
crash. My duties as management officer were extensive
and multifaceted: accommodate the more than 300
military personnel who flew in to launch the search and
rescue mission and set up a field hospital and morgue;*

173

> *attend meetings with Ethiopian officials; meet with the chief of mission and our embassy's Emergency Action Committee to manage not only our support to the search and rescue, and later the recovery mission, but also our own community's reaction; and keep the task force in Washington apprised of management activities and requirements in connection with the crisis. If I was lucky, I got four hours of sleep a day, and at the end of two weeks, I was exhausted and certainly not functioning at anything approaching full capacity. This crisis convinced me to follow steadfastly the guidance of crisis management experts in the subsequent crises: Eat, sleep, exercise.*

This heartbreaking account ends in "Eat, sleep, exercise"? Yes, it does, as crass as that might seem, because what we're going to talk about is the management of crisis, not its final consequences. I'm only going to say this once, right at the beginning of our meeting, because it's *really* important: You need to be at the top of your game throughout a crisis, not just going into it. Find time – *make time* – each day to eat well, get enough sleep or other concentrated form of physiological rest (such as meditation, a power nap, etc.), and get some physical exercise – walking, running, yoga, weights, or whatever the circumstances allow. Ignore the self-important, "Type A" folks running around implying that anyone who takes time for these things in the middle of a crisis is a slacker who is not fully committed to the cause. They're already off their game. *Eat, sleep, exercise!*

What is the international manager's role?

If you are both the head of your overseas operation and the person responsible for its administration, you will be in the driver's seat during a crisis. If you are not the head of the operation, you will still find that, as the person principally responsible for management and administration, you are going to play a central role in managing almost all crises that affect your overseas operation. Many other employees will play important roles, as well: security officers, public affairs officers, human resources officers, budget and fiscal officers, logistics officers, etc. These people might work directly for you or they might report to others in the organization. You will have to gauge your situation on the ground to figure out precisely where you fit in and how much control you have over the general management of the crisis. In my experience, however, the kinds of crises overseas operations experience are ninety percent management and ten percent policy, so it's pretty safe to assume that, as an overseas operations manager, you will be very much in the middle of things. I am going to proceed on that assumption.

The wise international manager contemplates and plans for crises. You obviously don't want one to occur at your overseas operation, but if one does, you certainly want to be as prepared as possible to deal with it. During this meeting, we're going to talk about how you can do that. We'll discuss the characteristics and range of crises that could affect your operation and the unique aspects of managing crises overseas. Thereafter, we'll then turn our attention to planning for crises. Please understand that this meeting is not a substitute for sound crisis or emergency planning; rather, my intention is to share with you some thoughts about what's important as you prepare for and guide your overseas operation through crises.

What is a crisis?

We could get into a lengthy philosophical discussion here if we tried to settle on a definition that suited all people in all circumstances, but that's not what we're going to do. Looking at this from the international manager's point of view, a crisis is a fundamental, often sudden, change of circumstances that significantly affects the people in your operation and alters the way you do business, temporarily or permanently. Crises can occur at several levels – personal, organizational, communal, national, regional, or international. Any of these might affect your operation.

> **Lilongwe, Malawi:** At 2:00 a.m. one morning, I received a call from the embassy's management officer advising me that one of our expatriate staff members had been involved in an accident and sustained life-threatening injuries. His Malawian girlfriend was also in the vehicle, although her injuries were not as serious. In very short order, we had to arrange for the medical evacuation of our staff member to South Africa, help his girlfriend obtain appropriate medical assistance locally, cover his function at the embassy until we could get additional support from Washington, and advise our embassy community before rumors started to fly about the employee's condition or the circumstances of the accident. Once it was clear that the

176

individual's injuries were too serious to allow him to return to post, we had to work with the State Department to have someone assigned to his position on a permanent basis and arrange to have his household effects packed and sent back to the United States. We also had to issue a reminder to the members of our community about the dangers of traveling Malawi's roads after dark. All the while, we were dealing with a community saddened by the tragic circumstances of one of its members and, of course, much other important work was pushed aside as we dealt with the entire situation. A personal crisis had become an organizational one.

Lomé, Togo: *One Saturday evening, I received a call from a United Nations colleague advising me that President Eyadema had died while being medically evacuated from Togo. Members of the diplomatic community were aware that the president had one or more serious medical conditions, but his death came as a surprise to us, and indeed to the Togolese public. We immediately convened the embassy's Emergency Action Committee to determine what effects the president's death was likely to have on public safety and our community. I put in a quick call to the State Department's Operation Center and advised appropriate Department officials of the situation. Contrary to Togo's constitution, after the prime minister announced the president's death, the Togolese Army swore its allegiance to the president's son, who assumed power, sparking demonstrations – some violent -- over the next few weeks. The embassy was in constant contact with its own community and the broader American community throughout this period, alerting them to stand fast (i.e., stay indoors, wherever they might be) when we caught wind of demonstrations. Togo's political crisis had become one for the embassy, and, in fact, for all foreign organizations in country.*

The list of things that might cause or constitute a crisis is nearly infinite: hurricanes, floods, earthquakes, plane crashes, coups, economic collapse, strikes, riots, automobile accidents, burglaries, major breakdowns of utilities, or sometimes just very bad behavior on the part of employees or their family members. In one of the countries in which I served, angry but painfully embarrassed host country citizens approached my organization to complain that one of our expatriate employees was luring young children into his house and engaging in sexual activities. At other overseas operations, I've had to deal with cases of child and spousal abuse. Crises can come from both predictable and unimaginable directions. Regardless of their cause, they disrupt your operation in ways that force you to respond, and they have profound effects on your organization's community.

How are Crises Different Overseas?

The definition of crisis that we've applied to the work of the international manager is also applicable to the work of domestic managers. There are, however, distinct differences in how one manages crises at home and abroad. These differences lie not only in cross-cultural factors, but also in what causes the crises, the extent to which they affect the organization, the resources available to address them, their impact on the operation's community, and the manager's responsibility to deal with them.

As we have emphasized, cross-cultural factors are always present when addressing management challenges overseas, and this is certainly true of managing crises. Different cultures respond to events in different ways. What constitutes a crisis in one culture might not be in another. In the United States today, the fact that your adult child is living with a partner out of wedlock may or may not be a crisis for your family. From society's point of view, it's probably not. That would not be the case in many, more additional cultures, where such a situation could result in very serious cultural sanctions for the individuals and families involved. Understanding the local culture, therefore, is vital in counseling your expatriate employees and family members as to what's acceptable and what's not. Failure to do so could result in a crisis for your organization and its members.

Beyond what different cultures might or might not consider a crisis, it's also true that what constitutes an appropriate response to a crisis varies from culture to culture, and this can present challenges in managing such situations. In the thick of a crisis, you might not see something like this coming at you.

> ***Addis Ababa, Ethiopia:*** *After the U.S. military found the Leland airplane and determined that there were no survivors, the next task was to recover the bodies. Sadly, the crash was so intense that what the military found were body parts rather than intact, identifiable bodies. Its recovery experts, including a forensic anthropologist, painstakingly tried to match body parts and put them in*

179

the 19 coffins the military brought with it. After about three days of this, however, I received a visit from desperate Ethiopian officials explaining that, in Ethiopian culture, family members begin to fast as soon as they receive word of a relative's death. They don't eat again until that person is buried. The Ethiopians whose relatives died in the crash, the officials advised me, were far more concerned about burying their relatives quickly than they were about ensuring that all of the body parts were correctly matched.

Understanding what people in the host country consider a crisis and how they might respond to various crises is easier said than done. That's why it is extremely important to have HCN employees and other host country contacts providing you guidance when you're managing a crisis.

Now let's look at some causes of crisis overseas. Many countries do not enjoy the political stability of the United States and other developed, industrialized countries. In many less stable countries, civil unrest, communal or sectarian strife, and demonstrations that become violent are not uncommon, and, in the absence of honest, effective public security services, the likelihood that they might affect your operation can be high. If you're in one of these less stable countries -- and sadly, their number is not small – you will have to spend more time considering the various political crises that might occur, what their effects might be on your operation, and how you can respond effectively.

Many countries are also fragile economically. When various events occur – natural disasters, civil strife, financial disruptions, epidemics, etc. – these countries don't have the public or private resources to address them, exacerbating the crisis. A country's poverty can also prevent it from developing or maintaining its critical infrastructure, including public utilities. A sudden loss of water or electrical supply – something that you might not plan for if managing an organization in the United States -- will throw your overseas operation into serious crisis if you haven't developed contingencies.

Addis Ababa, Ethiopia: Two weeks after I arrived in Addis Ababa as Management Officer of the U.S. Embassy, lightning struck the high-voltage transformer that linked the embassy compound to city power. Our entire compound electrical system was fried in the process. The State Department had spent two years designing and planning for replacement of the compound's antiquated system, but when we took the lightning strike, the contract and materials for this project were not in the pipeline. The outage left us with one small generator for the embassy's communication system and another for its commissary freezer. The rest of the compound, on which all of us worked and half of us lived, lay in darkness. For security, operational and quality of life reasons, this was a crisis. A damning and desperate cable to Washington got things rolling on that end, but a permanent solution was many months away. Meanwhile, working urgently, the embassy's exceptionally resourceful, if daring, Ethiopian electrician managed to rig up a temporary system, stringing high voltage cables through trees in a manner which would have given any U.S. building inspector a heart attack, but which put us back in business in a week's time. You can be sure that this electrician was at the top of my list when I sat down to write performance award nominations that year! When we finally replaced our electrical distribution, not one, but two very large generators were part of the new configuration.

If a country lacks the stability, resources and critical infrastructure to respond to emergencies and disruptive events effectively, that also means that you, the international manager, lack local access to these resources. If you're a manager in the United States, it would be prudent for you to develop a plan for dealing with an outbreak of the swine flu or some other epidemic. That plan might include procedural changes, such as how you deal with the public and advice to your staff to stay at home in the event that they experience certain symptoms. Unless you're at a very large organization, a school or an isolated site, your plan probably won't involve obtaining vaccines or actually

181

treating those who fall ill. You'll rely on public and private healthcare providers for those services. In many countries where you'll be serving as an international manager, however, you won't have that luxury, and you will have to develop and implement complex systems for obtaining the supplies and services you'll need to deal with a crisis from beginning to end with little local support.

I mentioned the impact on one's organizational community as an element of crisis. Typically, a domestic organization's community – at least that portion directly affected by an event – is smaller than is the case for many overseas operations, especially those with large numbers of expatriate employees. In the United States, there's usually a clear separation between work, home and community. I've met some of the people at the organization where my wife works, and she has met a few of the people I work with at the University of Texas. We've even attended and hosted social events with these two groups. That said, neither of us can say that a significant number of the other's colleagues or their family members is part of our regular social network or community. That's not an uncommon situation in today's mobile, dual career U.S. society.

Overseas – especially in developing countries that lack extensive cultural and recreational amenities – the organization is often both the center of one's professional and social universe. This is not an ideal to strive for – in fact, doing one's job successfully overseas ordinarily argues in favor of an extensive network of both professional *and* social contacts from the host country – but in some locations it is a natural and somewhat logical development. One works and plays with the same people and knows their spouses and children well due to regular interaction at recreational and social events, via the local international school, etc.

So turning back to crisis management, this greater integration of the overseas operation into not simply work, but also home and community, means that a crisis can have a more profound effect, directly or indirectly, on a larger number of people. An airplane accident that kills your colleague in a domestic organization will deeply sadden those of you who worked with that person. Your own family members might also be deeply affected if they happened to know the person who died. If not, they might feel sad in the abstract, but the incident

182

probably won't constitute a crisis for them. In contrast, at many overseas operations you can be sure that the effects of an accident or serious illness affecting one member of the community will extend beyond those who work with them in the office to their families and the broader expatriate community and, as a result, become a more profound crisis for the organization. This is clearly something that the international manager has to keep in mind when managing crises overseas.

> **Addis Ababa, Ethiopia:** *Returning once again to the Leland airplane crash, the U.S. military wanted to set up its field hospital and morgue on the embassy compound, because the embassy controlled access to that site and it provided immediate access to our communication system. We proposed, instead, setting these facilities up at the airport, controlled by the Ethiopian government, because embassy families lived on the compound, and the presence of a field hospital and morgue in their immediate line of site would simply be too upsetting to a community that was awaiting word about the fate of five of its members. When that word finally came and we learned that all on board the aircraft had perished, our Chief of Mission (COM) encountered the husband of one of the embassy victims at the front steps of the Chancery, where he broke the tragic news. The COM, recounting the tragedy later, recalled that one of his most poignant memories of the crisis involved my young daughter, who happened to be passing by at that moment with my wife and son. As the surviving husband's knee buckled and he broke into tears, the COM saw my children witnessing the scene and my daughter asking, "Mommy, why is Michael crying?" Our community took many months to heal from that crisis. Those of us who went through it together were closer as a result, but perhaps not surprisingly, those expatriate employees and family members who arrived at post after the crisis reported that they felt like "outsiders."*

Your organization's expatriate employees and their families are not only more integrated, as a community, than may be the case for a domestic organization, but they are also separated from family, friends, and a familiar culture from which they can draw comfort and stability in a crisis. If the crisis attracts international media attention and is reported back home, these families and friends are also going to be quite anxious to know what's happening. If your location is remote and information about events there is sketchy -- as it might be if the local government has not allowed independent media coverage – you're going to have people growing increasingly tense in country and back home. This is a situation for which you can plan in advance, and we'll discuss it again in a few minutes.

Finally, managing a crisis overseas is different for the same reason that managing the operation's expatriate employees is: the organization's duties don't stop at the office door. If an employee of a domestic operation has an accident in his or her own vehicle late one evening, it is not the domestic organization's responsibility to ensure that the individual receives proper medical attention. If a hurricane is headed for the coastal town where the organization's headquarters is located, or a demonstration will be taking place there, it's not the organization's responsibility to ensure that its employees' houses are properly secured, that it knows where all of its employees and their family members are, or that, should its employees or their family members suffer injury or worse in these events away from their place of work, they receive emergency medical attention. Overseas, these are things for which the operation and you, as its manager, are responsible. The 24/7 responsibilities the international manager bears, especially with regard to expatriate employees and their families, are even more acute during a crisis.

How Does the International Manager Plan for Crises?

Managing crises big and small demands clarity of thought, deliberateness of action, having the right people involved, giving careful consideration to effects on the community, and, to the extent possible, having a premeditated plan.

Your organization might already have its own crisis management handbook and plan format, in which case, you will want to ensure that your operation-specific version is up to date

184

and relevant to the current circumstances. If your operation does not have a plan and your headquarters does not provide a format or guidance in this regard, there is an emergency planning handbook and a model contingency plan available on the website of the Overseas Security Advisory Council (OSAC), a committee that fosters cooperation on security matters between U.S. businesses and the U.S. Department of State: https://www.osac.gov/ResourceLibrary/index.cfm?display=type &type=1003.

Since crises and overseas operations come in so many different shapes and sizes, it is impossible to provide an exhaustive list of subjects your plan should cover. In consultation with others at your overseas location – expatriate and host country national employees, as well as other expatriates in country, host country government and private sector contacts, etc. – you should identify some of the more obvious crises that might arise. Here are some questions that I would ask myself in either assessing the relevance of my operation's current plan or developing one from scratch:

- What types of natural disasters have historically affected the host country?

- Is our operation in an earthquake zone, flood plain, or other area prone to a particular type of natural disaster?

- Is the government stable? Is civil unrest likely? What form might it take?

- Are local security forces capable of maintaining law and order in the event of a crisis or an incident that could become a crisis?

- Is the economic and financial system stable and reliable?

- Are the medical facilities and services we would need to deal with an individual emergency or broader crisis available and of adequate quality?

Answers to these questions will inform your decision about the types of crises that are most important to plan for.

Several elements should be common to all crisis management: communications, assembling the right crisis management team, managing the effects of a crisis on the community, and managing public relations in connection with a crisis. Let's look at these in turn.

Communications

In the first instance, you want to ensure that staff and family members associated with your overseas operation know who to contact in the event of an emergency or crisis. This might differ by type of event – accident, break in, fire, natural disaster, etc. It's also possible that, depending on your location, the point of contact is not in your organization, but some external source of support, such as the fire or police departments. In many countries, however, government services, even for such emergencies, will be unreliable to nonexistent. The main point is that people in your operation know who to call, so you need to ensure that your operation provides them guidance in this regard.

What means do people in your organization have to communicate in the event of a crisis? Are they entirely reliant on the phone system (land line or mobile) or e-mail? What if these services are down? This is not an unrealistic scenario, and should it occur, you would be cut off from the very people you urgently need to communicate with, so this is obviously something you want to consider carefully in advance. Some organizations provide some or all of their employees two-way radios for emergency purposes, which can be effective, if costly and often difficult to maintain. How many people your operation has and how widely dispersed they are will affect what's necessary and what's possible. Many organizations establish phone trees or other cascading networks for ensuring that they can reach all members of their community in the event of a crisis or emergency situation. U.S. embassies and consulates establish warden systems for contacting all Americans that they know to be living in their districts, and if it's not one of these embassies or consulates that you're managing, you will want to ensure that they are nonetheless aware of any American employees and family members associated with your operation.

With whom do you need to communicate in a crisis? Much is going to depend on the nature of the crisis, but here is what I believe is a pretty good pecking order:

1. People who can respond immediately to mitigate the crisis. The appropriate "first responders" could be within your operation, in the host government or other organizations in the host country, at your headquarters, at some regional center, or elsewhere. In addition to first responders, wherever they might be, you need to let the head of your overseas operation, if you are not that person, know that a crisis has occurred or is in the making and continue to keep that person briefed as things unfold.

2. The employees and family members for whom your operation is responsible, whether expatriates or host country nationals. Who, in your community, the operation needs to contact and how quickly will depend on whether the evolving crisis affects them directly or not. A car accident or plane crash won't require immediate communication with your entire community, but an earthquake or developing riot in the vicinity certainly will.

3. Others who have an official need to know that a crisis of some sort is occurring. Very often, this will be headquarters. It might be easy to forget, in the thick of a crisis, that your headquarters is not only in a position to help you, but also needs to know that something has occurred so that it can respond to those who might make inquiries. In that regard, too, it's useful for you to know in advance who to contact in headquarters for various types of crises. Do you have a way of contacting these people when a hurricane has brought down the local telecommunications system?

4. "The folks back home." As I noted earlier, if a crisis receives international media attention and reaches the relatives and friends of your expatriate employees, they are going to be very anxious to find out what's happened to their loved ones. You don't want the operation to take this task on in the midst of managing the crisis, but you do want to urge your employees to

187

be contact their families back home to advise them of their status. In a world of widely available, inexpensive communication, this is often not difficult, unless communications systems are down. When they are, you'd better have a Plan B. In some circumstances, you might request that headquarters contact the family members of your employees or organize a hotline that they can call for information. Establishing such a system and contact information before crisis strikes obviates the need to address this problem among the many others that confront you in a crisis.

The Right Team

When a crisis occurs, or you see something on the horizon that could result in a crisis, step back, clear your head, and think comprehensively about who needs to be involved in resolving it. If it's an event that affects everybody at your operation, the list of those who need be involved is obviously going to be much larger than it might be if the crisis is on a smaller scale. It is for such operation-wide crises that many organizations establish formal emergency action or crisis response committees in advance, assigning each member a specific role and duties. If you've established a committee, and its members are aware of what's expected of them and what's available to them to perform their duties, you will save a lot of time and spare the operation confusion in the crucial, early hours of the crisis.

Some crises won't warrant the involvement of an entire team, but most will involve the need for funds, personnel actions, guidance on security issues and the dissemination of information. Just about every crisis I have been involved in has required support from my operation's budget and fiscal officer, human resources officer, security officer and public affairs officer, as well as the person we relied upon to provide information to the community about what was transpiring or had already occurred. As the manager of a crisis, you will be more effective if you bring those who might have to respond together from the start so that you can share all relevant information and they can coordinate their efforts. Unless there's a reason for confidentiality or tightly controlling information, err on the side of including more people rather than fewer. If it turns out you don't need them, then you will be guilty of wasting their time. If, however, you do, the consequences of not having enlisted their support and brought them up to speed early could be much more serious. Efficiency is often not a good thing to worry about in the thick of a crisis.

Addis Ababa, Ethiopia: *When the Leland airplane disappeared, I very quickly found myself responding to several demands at once, attending meetings at the airport and the embassy, obtaining landing clearances for several U.S. military aircraft, making arrangements to accommodate a couple of hundred military personnel, etc. I felt like it was all I could do just to write down the many things I had to take care of. Being relatively new to the Foreign Service, I was reluctant to ask for assistance beyond what was available within our embassy community, because I hadn't had time to think through who was going to do what and I didn't want to request that people be sent in on an emergency basis if I wasn't sure I could fully utilize them. By Day Two of the crisis, I realized I needed help...too late. Our embassy in Nairobi sent someone up quickly, which was extremely helpful, but I could have used three more people at that point. By the time we were able to get additional people into Ethiopia, we were over the hump of the crisis, but my conclusion, thinking back later, was not that I should have avoided requesting them, but that I should have done so earlier. That's a lesson I applied in subsequent crises. Forget the stiff upper lip, "go it alone" stuff: Ask for help early in a crisis.*

Community Impact

As we discussed earlier, if something is genuinely a crisis for your overseas operation, it is going to affect your community in one way or another, emotionally, operationally, or both. Some crises will put your entire community at risk, and in those cases one of your main concerns will be to ensure that

189

everyone is safe and secure. Other crises, like the plane crash in Ethiopia, might have a direct impact on some employees and family members and a strong but indirect effect on others. In still other crises, the principal effects might be on office operations, more typical of crises in a domestic workplace. Whatever the case may be, you need to think about who is affected, directly or indirectly, and what you and the operation need to do as a result to mitigate those effects.

It's relatively easy to provide information to your operation's employees. You can send out a group e-mail message, make an announcement over a public address system, if you have one, convene a quick meeting, or advise supervisors to pass on information. Generally speaking, information and guidance travel a lot better within the office than they do between office and home, and when you're overseas, this can be a problem, especially if the crisis poses a threat to family members as well as employees. It's never ceased to amaze me what employees in the fog of crisis forget to tell their family members, even when that information directly affects their safety and wellbeing.

With that mind, you should develop ways of ensuring that information and guidance that you need to pass to employees' family members actually reaches them. You have some options in that regard: 1) the head of the operation can convene a town hall meeting of employees and their family members to convey critical information and address their concerns, which could be many; 2) you can enlist the support of one of the family members, perhaps for pay, to serve as a liaison between the operation and its families; 3) if you have some alternative system of communication, such as a radio system, you can broadcast messages that people will hear in their homes. U.S. embassies and consulates often hold town hall meetings in the event of widespread crises that affect the resident American community broadly, so if your operation has a U.S. affiliation, make sure that the nearest embassy or consulate is aware of its presence so that you receive announcements about these events.

> **Lilongwe, Malawi**: *During Malawi's transition from decades of one-man rule to democracy, the soldiers of the Malawi Army (somewhat surprisingly a force for*

democracy) moved unilaterally to disarm the ruling party's paramilitary group, the Malawi Young Pioneers. The Young Pioneers headquarters was two doors down from the U.S. Embassy, with the ruling party's headquarters in between. Hours into the soldiers' operation, both headquarters were on fire and the Young Pioneers were on the run all over the capital city, with soldiers in hot pursuit firing weapons. Given the proximity of our embassy to the action, we were tied down for much of the day. Inside, we convened our Emergency Action Committee and each officer set about performing his or her specific duties. Our community liaison officer (a paid embassy spouse) was responsible for ensuring that we knew where all members of our community were and that we could communicate with them. Unfortunately, the heaviest fighting was taking place between the embassy and the international school on the opposite side of town, so it was impossible to retrieve our embassy children and situate them more safely at home until very late in the day. Nevertheless, constant contact between the embassy and the school, where we had permanently positioned an embassy radio, enabled us to manage the children's whereabouts and retrieve them when it was safe to do so. We were also able to keep all parents advised of the children's status, which helped to discourage them from running off to the school in a panic, right into the line of fire. We sent out frequent messages to the entire American community, embassy and private, throughout the crisis.

Lilongwe, Malawi: During Malawi's transition from decades of one-man rule to democracy, the soldiers of the Malawi Army (somewhat surprisingly a force for democracy) moved unilaterally to disarm the ruling party's paramilitary group, the Malawi Young Pioneers. The Young Pioneers headquarters was two doors down from the U.S. Embassy, with the ruling party's headquarters in between. Hours into the soldiers' *operation, both headquarters were on fire and the Young Pioneers were on the run all over the capital city, with soldiers in hot pursuit firing weapons. Given the proximity of our embassy to the action, we were tied down for much of the day. Inside, we convened our Emergency Action Committee and each officer set about performing his or her specific duties. Our community liaison officer (a paid embassy spouse) was responsible for ensuring that we knew where all members of our community were and that we could communicate with them. Unfortunately, the heaviest fighting was taking place between the embassy and the international school on the opposite side of town, so it was impossible to retrieve our embassy children and situate them more safely at home until very late in the day. Nevertheless, constant contact between the embassy and the school, where we had permanently positioned an embassy radio, enabled us to manage the children's whereabouts and retrieve them when it was safe to do so. We were also able to keep all parents advised of the children's status, which helped to discourage them from running off to the school in a panic, right into the line of fire. We sent out frequent messages to the entire American community, embassy and private, throughout the crisis.*

Clarity of guidance is extremely important in a crisis. Precisely what do you want to tell the members of your community? Sometimes, if the crisis has not or will not affect them directly – i.e., they haven't been or won't be in harm's way – the objective might be to control rumors, assuage concerns or help the community deal with grief. If, however, the crisis is ongoing and is affecting the community directly, then you or someone in the operation needs to provide very clear instructions: e.g., stay where you are, avoid the city center, have a suitcase and travel documents ready for each member of the family, report immediately to the operation's offices with all family members, etc. There should be no room for ambiguity or misunderstanding, and employees must understand that the operation expects them and their family members to follow the instructions. Those unaccustomed to overseas service and the dangers that are sometimes involved might find this uncomfortably directive, but in some crises these are life or death matters. Actually, this is something that should be made clear to employees at headquarters – in crisis management training or otherwise – prior to departing for their overseas assignment.

Public Relations

Some crises are internal enough that they might not attract attention from outside the organization, but in fact these are rare. More typically, either the cause of a crisis or its effects are going to reach beyond your operation and require some kind of interaction with the general public – in the host country, at home, or elsewhere – or some subset thereof. Virtually every crisis for which I have provided an example during this meeting required some management of relations with the public. The Leland airplane crash attracted international media attention and frequent press statements by the embassy's Public Affairs Officer as the crisis evolved. The disarming of the Malawi Young Pioneers likewise prompted several calls from international media outlets, as did the death of President Eyadema in Togo and the violent protests that followed. Even the automobile accident in Malawi made the local newspapers, and we had to deal with the family of our injured employee's girlfriend, who was also injured, in the aftermath of the accident.

Because it's likely that a crisis will not remain a strictly internal affair, if it even started as such, those running your operation need to think about public relations very early in the process of managing it. If your organization has someone explicitly responsible for public relations, that person needs to be part of the team managing the crisis. The time to think about a proper response to the media or members of the public is not when they've succeeded in reaching someone in your organization on the phone. The potential for saying something the organization will regret by doing so on the fly – especially in the heat of a crisis – is extremely high. Depending on the severity of the situation, you might think about asking headquarters to send you a public affairs officer from one of its other operations for the duration of the crisis.

193

Headquarters, too, could be receiving inquiries from the media and the public; thus the importance, as I mentioned before, of keeping people there thoroughly and regularly briefed about your situation. Public affairs professionals at headquarters can take a lot of heat off of the overseas operation by fielding these inquiries if they have good information. Those managing the crisis at the overseas operation need to think carefully about how they ensure that headquarters is getting regular reports, both for its own sake and for public affairs purposes. Depending on the complexity of the crisis, it might be worth assigning someone the explicit role of reporting to headquarters on a fixed schedule or when there are major developments.

When Does the Crisis End?

Crises are obviously of varying lengths, and it might be easier to identify the end of some than it is of others. But beware! Crises have lingering effects that might not be obvious to those managing them.

Addis Ababa, Ethiopia: The Leland airplane crash had many lingering effects, from community members dealing with the loss of five of our colleagues to a mammoth financial mess, the result of multiple U.S. military units ordering and obtaining aviation fuel and other services without providing the embassy proper accounting data. To deal with our community's profound grief, the Chief of Mission hosted a very touching memorial service at his residence, inviting all employees, Ethiopian and American, and our embassy family members. It was a cathartic event following an emotionally and physically exhausting two weeks, a chance for all of us to finally let the tears flow. My first order of business, after the service, was to ask the State Department to send in a budget and fiscal officer. That individual spent an entire month at the embassy sorting out the financial situation so that local vendors could be paid. And then, as I mentioned before, we had the feelings of isolation that some of the newcomers experienced when they arrived at

194

post after the big crisis. Ironically, we ended up having so many crises in Ethiopia, which was still engaged in a civil war, that it wasn't long before another one came along to draw in those who hadn't been party to the last.

As my example suggests, having some event that formally defines the end of a crisis can be very useful in allowing for catharsis and signaling that it is time to move on...back to normalcy, one hopes. After the upheaval in Malawi, associated with the disarming of the Malawi Young Pioneers, the ambassador held town hall meetings in the capital and the largest city to brief all Americans in country about the crisis and what he thought it meant in terms of Malawi's political situation and their personal security. The meetings also gave those in attendance a chance to provide us very useful feedback on how well the systems we had put in place to provide them information and guidance had functioned. In a similar vein, after-action meetings of your crisis management team are crucial and should take place as soon as possible after the crisis, while people's memories are still fresh and they haven't moved on to deal with the pile of regular work that accumulated during the crisis.

The other thing that you want to get to right away, before falling back into your normal routine, is the recognition of those who participated in the crisis response. If your organization has a formal award process, this is the time to use it liberally and generously. This is also the time for the ultimate head of your organization, back at headquarters, to weigh in with a robust "job well done," and if this is not forthcoming, then suggest to the head of your overseas operation that he or she quietly remind the appropriate people.

Formal events and processes – memorial services, town hall meetings, after-action sessions, award ceremonies, etc. – aside, employees and family members are going to process the events that have transpired each in his or her own way. This is a time to be on the lookout for behavior that suggests that someone in your community is still dwelling on some aspect of the crisis. It's a time to encourage sensitivity to the needs and feelings of others, and to the extent that it's possible in the wake of a crisis, it's a time to create breathing space so that people can reconnect with the families they have often been forced to neglect in the heat of the crisis.

Lilongwe, Malawi: *The day the Malawi Army disarmed the Young Pioneers, I was Charge d'Affaires, the head of the mission, because the ambassador was out of the country. I stayed at the embassy very late into the night, because things were still developing and I needed direct access to our communication system. From the roof of the Chancery, the Public Affairs Officer and I watched the Malawi Congress Party headquarters smoldering and tracer bullets lighting the sky from all directions. Two weeks later, when things had calmed down, I was sitting in my living room when my son, who was eight, came and snuggled up to me on the couch. It was clear that something was bothering him, so I asked him what was up. He recalled the night of the disarming, and told me he'd seen the tracer bullets from his bedroom window and had been frightened by them. "Were you scared because you thought they might hit the house?" I asked, to which he replied, "No. I didn't know where you were."*

196

4:00 p.m.	**Meeting with Ambassador Engle**
	Extreme Management

It's a marathon, not a sprint.

---The standard warning against burning out under the crush of work in a war zone

Baghdad, Iraq: *I survived the C-130's defensive corkscrew landing without losing my lunch. Now I found myself in the hot Baghdad night scrambling around a baggage pallet with the other passengers, all of us in helmets and heavy body armor, trying to identify and take possession of our bags. Over the din of the airplane's engines, which continued to spool, I heard someone right next to me shouting "Are you Ambassador Engle?" I answered in the affirmative, and the airman advised me, "Your birds are over here, sir." "Birds?" I replied. Helicopters. More than one? Two, for protection. Other passengers? "They're your birds, sir." With that, I quickly handpicked the number of people who would fit into these birds (Black Hawks, to be precise), and we were soon strapped in and nearly scrapping the tops of Baghdad houses as we headed for the infamous Green Zone, referred to locally as the International Zone or IZ. The helicopter lights out, a gunner at the ready on each side of the Black Hawk, and the strong backwash from the giant rotating blades above sandblasting my face, it*

197

occurred to me, to the extent that I could drive "All along the Watchtower" out of my head (thank you, Forrest Gump!), that this was to be no ordinary overseas assignment.

During this meeting, we're going to talk about a type of management that has regrettably become more common in recent years: management in non-permissive environments. A non-permissive environment – very often a war zone -- is one in which host country security forces and local contract guards cannot adequately ensure the safety of your organization's property and its people. To do so, you must engage the support of either heavily armed security contractors or military forces from outside the host country. The most obvious examples of non-permissive environments in the first decade of the 21st Century were Iraq and Afghanistan, but several other locations also fit the description: Eastern Congo, Somalia, parts of Pakistan, the Nigerian delta.   When you're in one of these locations, it's a whole new ballgame, which I refer to here as "extreme management." If this were a competitive sport or a television show, I suppose it would be called "X-Management." It would probably have very low Nielson ratings. For those actually engaged in it, however, this type of management is challenging and rewarding.

Getting Ready

Every new assignment requires preparation, and Tibor provided some very useful guidance in this regard in an earlier meeting. People assigned to positions in war zones and other non-permissive environments – where the threat to life and limb is by definition very, very high – need to take additional steps to prepare themselves and their families.

Let's start with families. Typically, assignments in these locations are "unaccompanied": You can't bring your family members. Some organizations might have arrangements that allow the spouse of an employee to fill a position at the unaccompanied location if the spouse is otherwise qualified, but the vast majority of people serving in non-permissive environments have left their families behind. Several questions then arise, which you, now the "X-Manager," need to have the answers to so that you can provide others at your "X-Operation" high quality, informed support:

- Does the organization provide support of any kind to the families who remain behind?
- Does it pay for families to move to the location where they will stay while the employee is on an unaccompanied assignment? Are there any restrictions with regard to support in this connection: E.g., the organization will pay to return family members to the city in which the organization has its headquarters, but not to other locations?
- Does the organization provide any allowance or salary supplement to offset the cost of maintaining a separate residence for one's family away from the employee's duty station?
- Does the organization offer special short courses, workshops or information sessions for families of those assigned to non-permissive environments? Such sessions might cover support from the organization, emergency contact information, and mental health guidance for coping with the separation and the fact that their loved one is in a dangerous location.

Separation from family members is one of the toughest things about serving in war zones and other non-permissive environments. As you will see, given the huge volume of work there is to do at X-Operations, the last thing you'll want is distracted expat employees. Thus, it's worth your while to encourage your organization to be supportive of families to the maximum extent and to ensure that incoming employees have availed themselves of organizational support and established comfortable arrangements for their families *before* they report for duty.

Beyond family concerns, there are several other preparations specific to service in non-permissive areas. Foremost among them should be special security training for high threat environments, to include information about the situation generating the threat, unique security practices in the assignment location, and perhaps even emergency first aid instruction. Employees bound for dangerous assignments should review their wills and life insurance policies to ensure that they are in order and appropriate to the higher threat environment in which they will be working. Does the organization offer any special provisions for supplementing or revising organization-supported insurance policies when one is assigned to a war zone?

Many organizations provide employees serving in non-permissive environments a range of benefits unique to that assignment: danger pay, special payments for what are typically much longer work schedules, additional leave time and R&R (rest and recuperation) travel, etc. Generally, it's headquarters job to advise employees preparing for these assignments as to any special benefits. The X-Manager should, however, ensure that this is taking place consistently and effectively. An uninformed expat employee on your doorstep will cost you precious time as you bring that person up to speed and walk him or her through filing required forms, etc. The U.S. Department of State established a special office through which people assigned to Iraq had to pass. They could not get approval to depart for post until that office was sure that they had gone through all of the necessary steps. This saved me a lot of time that I didn't have to waste as Management Counselor at the U.S. Embassy in Baghdad.

We've already spoken about making effective use of your consultation time and cultivating key contacts in your pre-departure time at headquarters. This will never be more important than when you're headed out as an X-Manager. Operations in war zones and other hostile environments are generally front and center on their organization's radar screen. As a result, it can feel like headquarters is always looking over your shoulder or on your back to provide more information about what's going on. In fairness, headquarters, too, is often feeding other masters – the White House or Congress, member states demanding information about what the UN field office in X is doing about the crisis at hand, donors of your NGO or humanitarian relief organization wanting to ensure that their money is making a difference. More than ever, you want to have effective relationships with the various people at headquarters who will be supporting you and to whom you have to report. Use your consultation time wisely!

Adjusting

Arriving at an assignment in a war zone is a disorienting experience. Most of us – most of us civilians, that is -- are not used to helicopters flying overhead day and night, heavily armored convoys, endless security checkpoints, people walking around with weapons, buildings surrounded by concrete T-walls or sandbags, etc. These physical manifestations of the extreme environment into which one has arrived are the most obvious, but for me, the real "shocker" in my first few weeks in Iraq was the quantity and pace of work. Given the high risk and the huge expense, organizations generally don't send more people into non-permissive locations than they think they need, and often the result is to send fewer people than might be required to accomplish the work that must be done. Thus, those on the ground at the X-Operation have to work long hours at a fast pace. In Baghdad, I worked from 7:00 a.m. to 9:30 p.m. or 10:00 p.m. (assuming there was no immediate crisis), seven days a week, and I was not alone. My observation was that people accomplished their work there at about three times the normal pace. Once I had adjusted my pace, I would lose my patience on conference calls with Washington, in which it seemed my

201

stateside colleagues wanted to discuss things endlessly. "We're done with that topic, I'm moving on," I would advise those at the other end of the line.

Such an intense work environment can seem chaotic and confusing at first. New arrivals are keenly aware that they're not getting a lot of what's going on around them. Seasoned veterans of the war zone (i.e., those who have been there for three weeks or more) are speaking in acronyms about subjects and developments the new arrival might have thought he or she understood prior to arrival. One can easily spot the "newbies": they're the ones with that classic "deer-in-the-headlights" look on their faces. Of course, as a newly arrived X-Manager, you will go through the same adjustment, but once you get through it, it's your job to help new arrivals adjust. It cost your organization a lot of money to get each expat employee to the   X-Operation, and it is strongly in your interest to see that each one succeeds.

> **Baghdad, Iraq**: *I counseled many new arrivals during my thirteen months in Baghdad, and my advice was consistent: "Don't make any judgments about the place, your work, or yourself during your first three weeks at post. Everything will seem out of focus during this period, because you have indeed come to a place that does not function much like any other place you've been.   Just observe and go with the flow.   In about two or three weeks, things will start to come into focus as you figure out what's important and how things are done. If things become very clear, you've over-focused; it's really not that clear here."*

Surviving

Most people who volunteer to serve their organizations in non-permissive locations do, in fact, make the adjustment to the intense atmosphere and the quantity and pace of work. Nevertheless, the X-Operation's senior management must remain constantly vigilant to ensure that the work environment is as supportive as possible.   One of the greatest dangers is not physical injury or worse as the result of an attack, but rather mental burnout. Working day in and day out seven days a week causes one to lose track of time. Each day seems like the last, and it can feel as if time is not passing at all. In Baghdad, we called this the Groundhog Day Syndrome after the movie in which Bill Murray lives the same day over and over again. Endless work with no sense of time can be extremely disorienting, affecting one's performance.

> ***Baghdad, Iraq:*** *The Deputy Chief of Mission (the embassy's #2) and I conducted regular town hall meetings with different groups of embassy employees to find out how they were doing. In our first meeting with the untenured (junior) officers, we asked them what caused them the most stress, naively assuming they would mention something about the dangerous security situation: mortar and rocket fire into the IZ, riding in armored convoys in the Red Zone, etc. Much to our surprise, they did not mention these things. Instead, at the top of their list of concerns was burn out, and they expressed the wish that they could spend just a few hours a week doing something other than work without feeling like they were slacking.*

One thing senior management can do to alleviate the fog and anxiety of the Groundhog Day Syndrome is to insist that employees take at least one day a week off to get some badly needed rest and vary their routine. This is easier said than done, because people are so busy, but doing so should produce a healthier, more productive team. In addition, senior managers should ensure that the organization has a robust R&R program for people serving at the X-Operation, strongly advocating for the same, if it doesn't exist. They should further insist that employees actually take the R&Rs to which they are entitled. Effective management demands that nobody is in fact indispensable, such that he or she can't get away for a periodic dose of the real world (the non-permissive environment is NOT the real world). If necessary, senior managers must take steps to force individuals who have designated themselves indispensable to get out and get real.

Confronting Unique Management Challenges

There are several management challenges that are unique to non-permissive environments and unaccompanied assignments. They can rule the X-Manager's life.

Expat Staffing

One of the first questions that arises when considering how to staff an operation in a non-permissive location is whether to do so strictly on the basis of volunteers or impose a requirement that employees of the organization serve there. Service in Iraq and Afghanistan is not voluntary for members of the U.S. military, but for most civilian agencies, it remains so. Some organizations, depending on how they staff themselves generally, would find it very difficult to require their personnel to serve in a war zone or other dangerous location.

If an organization's staffing policy for X-Operations is based on voluntary service, how large is the pool of employees who are willing to leave their families and work for some period of time in a place that is, by definition, dangerous? If the number of current employees willing to serve is less than the number necessary to accomplish the work on the ground, is the organization willing – and does it have the means and mechanisms – to hire people from outside the organization to fill these positions? What happens when the organization has cycled through its pool of those willing and available to serve?

How long should the assignment to a non-permissive location be? There's tension here between the need to adjust to the quantity, pace and complexity of the work in this environment and the risk of burning out. The organization wants employees to stay long enough to learn the ropes and contribute positively to the work of the X-Operation, but not so long that they wear down and lose "real world" perspective, rendering them less effective. In addition, given the fact that assignments to these field operations are usually unaccompanied, there's a direct relationship between the length of separation from family and the willingness of people to volunteer for such service. As a result of these tensions, assignments to non-permissive locations are typically shorter than regular overseas assignments, often by half or more.

Shorter assignments have a direct impact on managing the X-Operation, forcing headquarters, the X-Manager, or probably both, to perpetually recruit. In Baghdad, the Deputy Chief of Mission and I, working closely with the State Department, conservatively spent 20 percent of our time identifying and recruiting candidates to serve in Iraq. That's a time sapper in a situation where demands for senior management's attention in other areas are also extreme.

Another downside to shorter assignments is limited institutional memory. If 90 percent of expat employees rotate out every year, taking into account the few who opt to extend, historical understanding of the X-Operation's policies, programs and procedures is going to be much thinner that it would be at an overseas operation where the standard assignment is two to four years and expat employees rotate in and out on a more staggered basis. As we've discussed, host country national (HCN) employees play a very important role in preserving institutional memory, but as we'll see in a minute, there are reasons why this might not be quite as true at X-Operations. One means of achieving better continuity as expat employees transfer in and out more frequently is to insist upon an overlap of at least a week between a departing employee and that person's replacement. During this period, the former can fully brief the latter concerning ongoing activities and developments and the latter can pose questions directly to the departing employee.

The HCN Dilemma

Whether one works for a diplomatic, international, non-governmental or commercial organization, it is very often the case that HCN employees outnumber expat employees by a considerable margin. As Tibor explained in your meeting on this subject, these employees typically provide the continuity and institutional memory in overseas operations. Hiring HCNs to do the same at the X-Operation is an attractive possibility. They know the lay of the land, which in this case is some pretty hostile territory. They are already at the location into which it's difficult and costly to bring expat employees. The organization often does not have to provide them housing and services, saving tens of thousands of dollars.

The benefits are obvious. So what are the issues? Let's just start hiring HCNs to perform as many functions as possible. Well...that might be the right course of action IF your organization is in no way associated with whatever has rendered the location non-permissive and thus working for it does not pose a threat to potential HCN employees. In Iraq, the U.S. Embassy and its affiliated agencies could not satisfy those conditions: They were indeed associated with the conflict and working for them could put the lives of Iraqis and their families in danger. So what about American NGOs and other organizations that did not work directly for the embassy? Their U.S. affiliation was still a problem, as a series of kidnappings and attacks on both expat and HCN employees of such organizations demonstrated. How about U.N. offices and affiliates? Same problem. In fact, one of the most devastating attacks on foreigners in Iraq was the bombing of the U.N. country office, in which its Resident Representative and many other U.N. employees, foreign and Iraqi, were killed. During the worst years of the insurgency in Iraq, it was the rare foreign organization, especially of non-Middle Eastern affiliation, which escaped the unwanted attention of extremists and insurgents.

The problem, in this case, is often not a shortage of HCNs who would like to work for your X-Operation, but rather the threat they face when they do and the problems such threats pose for the organization. Foreign organizations tend to pay well and offer much needed employment in an economy that has been battered by war or conflict. So desperate are local people to find employment and provide for their families, that they are willing to risk life and limb to do so. Successfully employed by the foreign organization, they will go to great lengths to keep their employment a secret from all but one or two of their closest relatives. They might spend hours commuting circuitously to and from work to avoid direct association with their foreign employer, and if the organization is housed in something akin to Baghdad's International Zone, they might spend hours just waiting in line for inspection and permission to enter. There may be days when they can't show up at all, because they have reason to believe they have generated suspicion, or there may be a security incident that cuts off their access to the foreign organization. It might be difficult for them to be seen in public with officials of their organization.

There is yet another problem with hiring HCNs in non-permissive environments: The X-Operation might find it difficult or impossible to run thorough and reliable background checks on HCN applicants. The organization cannot brush this deficiency aside lightly, given the real possibility that those who would do it harm could take deadly and destructive advantage of the situation. Under such circumstances, the X-Operation is likely to be much more cautious about the functions it has its HCN staff performing, as well as the access it grants them to information that could jeopardize the security of its personnel, property and programs.

For all of these reasons, HCN employment in non-permissive locations is more problematic than it is elsewhere, and as a result, many X-Operations have far fewer HCNs relative to expat employees than would normally be the case. As I mentioned above, this makes it harder to rely on HCNs to provide the institutional memory that is generally their stock in trade. It also means that, both for the sake of the organization and the HCNs who are risking their lives to work for it, the X-Manager must keep a close eye on compensation levels, benefits and security practices that affect HCNs to ensure that the organization is taking care of them in the best way possible under very difficult circumstances.

One means of addressing the HCN dilemma is to hire third country nationals (TCNs) from neighboring countries to perform tasks that HCNs might otherwise perform. The objective would be to hire individuals who speak the local language and have a good working knowledge of the culture, but whose profile in the host country is limited: They are unknown to the local community and their families are safely outside the country. The threat against the TCN could be lower and more manageable than that against the HCN. The downside is that the costs of TCN staffing are inevitably higher, because the organization has to pay to transport them into and out of country, house them at the X-Operation, and most likely provide them danger pay to serve in the non-permissive environment. Thus, TCN hiring is not a panacea, but it is an option when HCN staffing proves too complicated in terms of the organization's operations and too costly in terms of the threat to those hired.

207

Security

We defined the no-permissive environment as one in which host country security forces – the police and the military – and local contract guards cannot provide an adequate level of security to the organization's personnel, property and operations. How then does the X-Operation achieve this "adequate level of security"?

The answer to this question varies greatly depending on the type of organization involved. Some organizations might have a legitimate claim to security support from a foreign security force in country. The U.S. Embassy in Iraq received much of its security from the U.S. military, which, along with other coalition military forces, secured the International Zone. In fact, every entity inside the IZ benefitted from this protection. This included Iraqi government offices, several other embassies, UN offices, some NGOs and thousands of private Iraqi residents. Organizations located outside the IZ constantly made the pitch to move inside.

If your organization has no clear basis for requesting security support from some resident military or other government-sponsored armed force, you might have to make private security arrangements, and in a war zone, these will be extremely costly. There are now a multitude of private security firms providing the heavily armored support an organization often needs to protect its facilities, staff and movement in non-permissive environments. The rules and conditions under which they operate, including their use of force, is an evolving issue. You might recall the 2006 incident at a Baghdad traffic circle in which a protective security detail operated by a U.S. contractor opened fire in response to a perceived threat, killing 17 Iraqis civilians. The nature of support an organization might need in this connection depends on the extent to which it might be a target of local combatants, terrorists or insurgents. Some organizations enjoy a certain level of local protection, even from insurgents, if those engaged in the fight perceive them to be either neutral or doing good work on behalf of the local population. That's an assessment senior management should reach only after careful consideration of all factors and in consultation with a number of expert sources, including experienced security professionals. There are too many

208

examples of NGO and humanitarian relief workers being taken hostage or attacked in Iraq, Afghanistan, Somalia, Sudan and elsewhere to make the blind assumption that non-governmental or humanitarian status wraps an organization in a bullet-proof mantel of protection from local insurgents and extremists.

Beyond ensuring that the X-Operation enjoys an adequate level of security protection, its senior management must be sure that there are security procedures in place that the organization's employees know well and observe when an incident occurs or the organization receives credible threat information. A war zone is no place for sloppy security practices. When the "duck and cover" alarm goes off, because, for instance, indirect mortar or rocket fire has struck the area or is incoming, you need to know that your X-Operation's employees are ducking and covering accordingly. What is the organization's policy with regard to employees who fail to observe these procedures?

Logistics for Hire

In a non-permissive environment, it is generally not the case that an organization can send its people around town to buy everything they need to keep the operation running. Many field operations in non-permissive locations are start-ups, which their headquarters have established specifically in response to the crisis situation on the ground, so in fact their needs are very great. If many goods and services are not available on the battered local economy, and it is too dangerous to be out looking for them in any case, how do X-Operations get what they need? One answer is logistics contractors.

The U.S. military has made extensive use of logistics contractors for many years. Serving the military, U.S. government civilian agencies, other countries' governments, the UN system, NGOs and commercial firms, a growing number of companies with international operations have developed the capacity to erect and manage offices and residential quarters, run dining and laundry services, operate freight transportation systems, and even provide morale support facilities and activities – all in the middle of a war zone. Obtaining logistical services via one of these companies can make it easier to establish one's X-Operation, but these services come at a very high cost. The alternative is for the organization, on its own, to figure out how to house, feed, supply and maintain itself; this might be easier for smaller organizations better able to live off of what they manage to obtain locally than for larger operations that require great volumes of goods and supplies.

It's very important for the X-Manager to understand thoroughly his or her options for obtaining logistical support, furnishings, equipment and provisions. Some logistics contracts are on a cost-plus basis, which means that the contractor receives some defined percentage above the cost of providing goods and services. Contractors sometimes enjoy considerable leeway under the terms of these contracts to determine what to provide and how to provide it. This makes sense in the start-up phase of operations, when people at the X-Operation are fully engaged in the activities for which the operation was established and don't want to be distracted by logistical issues. It makes less sense, in my opinion, when the X-Operation is up and running and its requirements are more predictable and routine. At that point, the X-Manager should start looking for functions to take over from the effective but highly costly logistics contractor, who has no incentive to keep costs down under a cost-plus contract.

> **Baghdad, Iraq:** *One morning, while walking from my trailer to "the Palace," i.e., the Republican Palace which served as the U.S. Embassy and MNF-I forward headquarters, I noticed a crew tearing up the sidewalk near one of the water points where a small forklift delivered cartons of bottled water on a daily basis. Over the next few days, the project got bigger and bigger, until the crew was pouring ten inches of concrete into a huge foundation, much larger than the original sidewalk, lined with heavy reinforcement bars. The resulting expanse of concrete was strong enough and nearly large enough to land a helicopter on. Perplexed, I asked my management staff if anybody knew what the project was about and why a small water point was suddenly a landing pad. Nobody knew. I insisted on an explanation and learned that the contractor had purchased (at what cost I shudder to think) a very large new forklift with which to deliver water, and that the "landing pad," at a cost of $22,000, was to support it. Very shortly thereafter, I convened a*

210

meeting with those supervising the contract and demanded greater oversight over new projects and how the contractor executed them.

Too Many Zeroes

Given the overall cost of operating the U.S. Embassy in Baghdad, the $22,000 I mentioned in the foregoing vignette was "chump change." In fact, the embassy's task order under the Department of Defense's logistical contract was chump change relative to the entire contract, and Department of Defense personnel sometimes questioned why I "wasted" my time chasing down such "small" savings. Part of the reason was that I came from an organization that was chronically short of funds for its worldwide operations, and spending money carelessly was irresponsible, even in a war zone. The other reason was my concern that unnecessary projects of smaller scale raised the

211

possibility of the same on a larger scale, costing the embassy much larger sums. By imposing greater control, with some bluster, I signaled a determination to contain logistical costs.

Aside from danger and risk, the thing that most characterizes management of X-Operations is X-Costs: the cost of operating in a non-permissive environment can be astronomical. The only way I maintained my sanity when looking at cost figures in Baghdad was to train my eyes to eliminate the last three zeroes. In addition to logistics contracts, the principal drivers of these extreme costs are security and the need to import so much of what an organization needs. In fact, these two factors are related: it's very expensive to bring in contract security personnel and equipment from outside the non-permissive location, and where attacks on supply convoys are frequent, these security personnel and equipment are needed to protect the importation of other goods and supplies, which raises their costs.

The responsible X-Manager must constantly search for potential savings. That means not only reviewing management, contracting and procurement practices, but also taking a careful look periodically at the X-Operation's staffing, which is another major cost driver. Do all of the expat employees really need to be in country? Could any of them perform their functions from headquarters or some regional location? A smaller staffing profile could reduce the need for logistical and security support, further reducing costs. This is not to suggest that the field operation should reduce its staffing to the point where it can't meet the objectives for which headquarters established it, simply that reviewing operations and their effects on cost drivers is an ongoing responsibility of the X-Manager.

Two Closing Thoughts

Earlier, we discussed the importance of making comfortable arrangements for one's family before departing on an assignment to an unaccompanied location. There is also a need to establish a means and routine for communicating with one's family – to include one's parents, spouse, children and siblings – while one is in a non-permissive environment. You tend to worry less about yourself, even in a dangerous situation, than do your family members. You know what's going on around you; they don't. All they know, aside from what you tell them, is what they pick up in the news: "Several rockets landed in Baghdad's Green Zone today." Best to stay in close touch so that they don't spend too much time worrying needlessly.

Keeping an X-Operation running effectively, as an X-Manager, can be X-tremely challenging and X-hausting. It can also be X-hilerating and X-traordinarily rewarding. Okay, enough with the X's. But seriously, if an organization has established a field operation in a war zone or other non-permissive environment, at great expense, it is obviously a high priority. It is eminently clear, when you're serving there, that headquarters considers your work very important, and its desire to support you and the activities of the X-Operation is high. In addition, most of the people with whom you serve in the non-permissive environment are dedicated individuals who, like you, want to make a positive difference in a bad situation. Serving your organization with such people in such an intense situation is a rare opportunity and an experience you will never forget.

4:45 p.m.   *Meeting with Ambassador Engle*
The Send Off

He didn't have 23 years of experience; he had one year of experience repeated 23 times."

---A former boss of one of the authors describing someone who failed miserably as an international manager

Well, you've had a full day of meetings. We could continue to regale you with war stories about managing organizations overseas, but, beyond what we've already shared, this would serve little purpose. You will learn this trade in the field. Some of your success will depend on what you know – about your organization and its objectives, the country you're serving in, etc. – but much more will depend on the quality of your judgment, and that develops with experience. You will make mistakes; learn from them! Don't be the manager with one year of experience repeated 23 times.

There is no single template for managing all overseas operations. An NGO with one expatriate, as director for instance, is going to look and feel very different from a large embassy with over 100 expat employees. The country office of an international organization, with staff members from multiple countries, is going to have unique advantages and challenges not shared by the NGO or the embassy. That said, there will also be many factors in common, and it is those we have tried to focus on during our "meetings" today. We believe that simply being

215

aware of some of these dynamics will give you an edge in addressing the challenges that will no doubt present themselves, nearly from the moment you arrive in country.

Countries, too, are very different from one another, of course. We've talked about a variety of cultural factors, and it is indeed important that you learn as much as you can about the place where you're living and working. In my experience, differences between countries have at least as much to do with their level of development or the extent to which they are traditional or modern societies than with the specific region in which they're located. Throughout our meeting we have been inclined to discuss our experiences in developing countries, generally with traditional cultures, because these are not only more different from the United States than developed countries with modern cultures, but also because the former tend to present the biggest challenges to the international manager.

A corollary of each country being different is that each overseas assignment is different. Even in organizations, such as U.S. embassies, which operate according to worldwide standard operating procedures, one post is going to feel very different than another. The local scene and cultural environment, as well as the personalities within the overseas operation, will ensure that this is the case. The lesson, then, for the new international manager is first not to judge service in the organization by one assignment, and second, not to assume that the challenges and solutions of one's last assignment will apply to the next one. The international manager must remain flexible, open, and always ready to learn new tricks.

My Best Advice

Rather than simply review the broad topics and issues that we discussed in our earlier sessions, let me use these last few minutes to share with you some even broader advice that I think is of particular relevance to the new international manager. I put this advice together a few years ago when my son was about to take his first professional position. At the request of colleagues, I've subsequently shared it with the staffs of the offices for which I've worked at the University of Texas. If you're closer to the beginning of your professional career, you might find the advice more personally applicable, but that doesn't let

216

those of us who are further along in our careers off the hook; in fact, I still have to remind myself of these points. In any case, the seasoned manager might find the advice useful in mentoring more junior colleagues. This advice is also equally relevant to expat and host country national employees.

So here we go:

There are no problems, just solutions. If you have to approach your boss for guidance on a problem – and you will – be sure that you also propose solutions.

Take your work seriously, but don't take yourself *too* seriously. People who take themselves too seriously aren't much fun to work with and typically have less support from others than they think they do.

Be reliable! If you commit yourself to do something, do it. Get the job done, and do it well, consistently. You want your boss to tell others, "I know I don't have to look over _____'s *[your]* shoulder."

Carry something to write with. Almost nobody's good enough to remember everything others have asked him or her to do, and asking your boss for something to write with makes you look unprepared.

Be on time to meetings. It's disrespectful to waste other people's time by making them wait for you (and this applies to senior people as well as junior ones).

Be a high productivity/low maintenance employee. Be genuinely enthusiastic about your work. That spirit will infect others. Show initiative. Be a self-starter. Take a little bit of guidance and run with it. But don't hesitate to ask if you really need advice or clarification; it's better than going down the wrong track. *But remember to propose solutions, as well!* **Leave the drama at home!** Don't crave attention. Always assume your bosses are busier than you are. That's normally a safe assumption.

Be a team player. Help the team and each member in it. People really appreciate someone who sincerely cares about helping other people deal with problems and succeed. Don't compete with other people – compete with yourself; be the best you can be. Know what the organization's goals are and add value to the organization by playing your part in achieving them. If you really want to be of value to your organization, figure out what others there dread doing (international management tasks typically fit this description!) and learn to do it well and with enthusiasm. They will love you for it.

Follow your boss's lead. Figure out what your boss likes or dislikes (in terms of how people work and communicate with him/her) and adjust your work habits accordingly. Each boss has a different style of working. They all want just the right amount of information, but what they define as "just right" will vary greatly. You want your boss to say of you, "[He/she] knows exactly what to bring to me and what to deal with on [his/her] own." Bosses all have one thing in common: they call the shots, because they're ultimately held accountable for the performance of their unit. Bosses are not always right. Figure out how to suggest other courses of action to your boss if you think that what he or she is doing will have a negative result. BUT don't be determined to change your boss's behavior or decision; don't wrestle with your boss. Once your boss makes a decision, carry it out sincerely and with a desire to achieve the result he or she wants.

Don't compromise your moral or ethical principles. If your boss is doing something unethical or morally wrong, and you can't live with it (Good for you!), either be prepared to suffer the negative consequences of challenging it (perhaps by bringing it to the attention of higher ups) or by finding another position. Fortunately, this sad situation doesn't occur very often.

Don't know? Don't fake it. Find out! It's okay to tell your boss or another senior officer in the organization that you don't know the answer to something they've just asked you. That's much better than trying to fake it, but the next words out of your mouth should be, "But I'll find out and get right back to you." Then do so.

218

Seek genuine feedback. In many organizations, written evaluations are inflated: be careful not to believe that you really do walk on water. Don't expect a lot of feedback and don't be a self-promoter. If you're doing really well, you'll normally get positive feedback without asking for it. Most bosses hate giving negative feedback, but in fact that feedback can be the most valuable. One way to obtain constructive criticism without making your boss feel uncomfortable is to ask her or him how you might best invest your energy to improve your skills or performance. That puts a positive spin on an otherwise awkward subject.

Keep your cool and be professional. Don't lose your temper. You will almost always regret having done so. Losing your temper in many foreign cultures can greatly reduce your effectiveness. The few times I've done so have been personal failures. If your temper does get the better of you, apologize to those who were affected, even if you think they caused you to lose your temper in the first place.

Be flexible and have a "can do" attitude. Most supervisors really get irritated by employees who feel that everything they do has to be written in their position description. If it's not, they'll refuse to do it. Very unhelpful! No task is too small or too low to do if it needs to be done to help the organization achieve its objectives.

Don't be hard on yourself. You're going to make mistakes. Analyze each mistake and learn from it. Then "get back on the horse" and keep working. If you make a mistake that is likely to have negative consequences for the organization, let your boss know right away and seek his or her guidance. Be honest and up front. Trying to cover up a mistake like this will almost always make matters worse.

Choose your battles carefully. Disagreements about courses of action are routine in the work place. If you fight every battle to the death, people will simply consider you combative and not take your arguments seriously. A few things may be worth fighting for even if you're going to lose – just on principle. *Simply proving that you're right is never one of them.* Figure out what's really important, but also figure out how you can bring your opponents on board. It's a give-and-take process, and success will be more lasting and rewarding if you can achieve a win-win solution.

Object without being objectionable. Disagreements are a natural part of professional work. When you get involved in one, keep it substantive and not personal. Your self-worth as a human being is in no way tied to whether or not you prevail.

Show respect. Every human being deserves her or his dignity. Never attack someone on a personal level, for the purpose of causing him or her to lose face in the eyes of others. *This is especially true overseas, where you are a stranger to the culture and may cause more harm than you know.* Some respect derives from one's position – where it is in the organizational order and what that means in terms of the responsibilities and authorities and how people interact with the person in that position. Even if a *position* commands respect, the *person* in the position must earn the respect of others. Respect is always a two-way street:

The respect that you expect others to pay you and that which you show to others are two sides of the same coin.

Communicate. It's a question of good manners and respect. If someone leaves you a message, get back to them as soon as you can. If someone sends you an individual e-mail (junk mail excluded), send them a timely reply. If you don't yet have the information necessary for an informative reply (or the time to draft one), send them an interim reply to let them know you've received their message and will provide them a more complete response as soon as you can. Not replying to messages generates uncertainty, concern, hurt feelings, etc.

Don't be more trouble than you are worth. No matter how much "superstar" status you have within your organization, there are limits to how much pain, drama, etc., you can cause for your bosses. You don't want to find those boundaries by being recalled to headquarters or politely shown the exit door.

Bon Voyage

I think I can safely speak for Tibor, as well as myself, in saying that the rewards of a career in international management are so great that neither of us would have traded our career in that field for any other. Were there frustrations? You bet! Were there days of heart-wrenching crisis? Yes; we both lost dear colleagues to service overseas, and we both saw local people living from day to day in dire poverty. But what was true through all of that was that, in positions of responsibility, as managers controlling human and other resources, we could take actions that made things better, and the tougher and poorer the location, the truer this was. I never once questioned whether the work I was doing overseas as an international manager was useful and important. Beyond that sober assessment, the work was also tremendously interesting and enjoyable, and I suspect, given my interests, I would have had trouble duplicating those rewards as a manager in a domestic organization.

So, all the best in your assignment as an international manager. You will get out of it what you put into it. To all of this I have only one more thing to add, a little mantra that served me well during my many years overseas:

Be flexible.

Keep your sense of humor.

Have fun!